TOWARD THE WESTERN OCEAN

❖ ❖ ❖

Toward the
Western Ocean

THE STORY OF THE MEN WHO
BRIDGED THE CONTINENT
1803 - 1869

by Albert Britt

BARRE PUBLISHING COMPANY
BARRE, MASSACHUSETTS
1963

In memory of
Nina
the patient listener

ILLUSTRATIONS

Following page 54

The illustrations are from periodicals in the collection of the American Antiquarian Society and are used with their permission.

CONTENTS

❖ ❖ ❖

For two hundred years the dream of a "Western Ocean" haunted the minds of Westward wandering Americans. They were a motley lot, those prisoners of a dream: explorers, fur traders, Mountain Men, missionaries, Mormons, gold-hunters, families in covered wagons. But they beat a way through mountains and deserts and hostile savages; they had courage and the strength to endure — until the Golden Spike was driven at Promontory Point and the old dream was fulfilled.

Albert Britt
Wellington Farm
Nonquitt, Massachusetts

❖❖❖❖❖❖❖❖❖❖❖❖❖❖❖❖❖❖❖❖❖❖❖❖❖❖❖❖❖❖❖❖❖

CHAPTER I

Westward Ho!

T HE YEAR 1862 was an important one in the
history of America. The war between North and
rendered Fort Sumter, the first battle of Bull Run had
ended in panic flight, and Lee seemed unbeatable. Appomattox and victory for the Union were three years away
and men were saying that the war was a failure and Lincoln
a stupid blunderer, but it was not the bungled battles and the
tragic lists of casualties that made 1862 important. This was
the year that Congress passed and the President signed two bills:
the Pacific Railways Act and the Homestead Act. The war,
desperate as it was, would end and the Union would be preserved; these two acts marked a beginning of new things, perhaps the most portentous in our history. The Railways Act
cleared the way for the building of a railroad from a place
called Council Bluffs to the Pacific Ocean. The Homestead
Act guaranteed settlers on the land who might one day become customers for the railroad.

Historical events, however sharply defined they may seem
at the moment, are deeply rooted in the past. The Northwest,
toward which these two bills passed in 1862 were aimed, had
been known and traversed by many men seeking many things

— furs, gold, adventure, freedom, land. British, French, Spaniards, Russians and Americans had looked at this country with envious eyes for nearly a century; more than that if Captain Cook's voyages are included. Captain Gray of the *Columbia* out of Boston had found a great river and named it for his ship, although an American poet christened it Oregon. Lewis and Clark blazed a trail from the Missouri to the Pacific. Fur traders and trappers had followed close on the heels of the explorers, and Mormons, gold hunters, and people in covered wagons had come that way. There is considerable mystery about the origin and meaning of the word Oregon. Milo M. Quaife, a careful student and a reliable editor, notes that Rogers the Ranger had used it after the Seven Years War when he was trying to organize an expedition to search for a Northwest Passage. Jonathan Carver, not always reliable, also used it in his "Travels," published in 1778.

In spite of their knowledge of the vast extent of the country lying to the westward of their possessions in Canada, the early French explorers had no adequate idea of the size of the Rocky Mountains and their difficulties. All of them, even Verendrye who was one of their best, thought of the Rockies as a single narrow chain with few high peaks and many easy passes. Immediately beyond this trifling barrier was the Pacific Ocean. They were equally mistaken in their estimation of the course of the Missouri River, placing it much too far to the south, perhaps even close to Santa Fe. Neither French nor Spanish had any conception that in places the main range was over two hundred miles in width, not including auxiliary chains and branches. The Spanish in Santa Fe were in constant expectation of the appearance of a French force threatening their hold on the Southwest. When they picked up Zebulon Pike and his men in Colorado they charged him with being an agent of the dreaded French. That was in 1806. Neither French nor Spanish had any concept of the extent and difficulties of the country lying west of the Rockies before they could sight the Pacific. There was general belief in the existence of a waterway to the western ocean. Even Jefferson, one of the best geographers of his time, shared this illusion and included the discovery of such a route in his instructions to Lewis and Clark.

Sir Francis Drake, a typical Elizabethan combination of fighting captain and pirate, cruised along the Pacific Coast, perhaps some distance north of Yerba Buena, as the Spanish called San Francisco harbor, but his interest was in fighting and loot and he neither knew nor cared about the American Northwest. Much later Captain Cook had a look in at Puget Sound; but on the other side of the continent the English were strangely tardy. By the time they made their first feeble gesture at settlement the Spanish were firmly established in the Southwest and the French in the North.

By the time the English came these two continental powers had been anchored in the new world for a long time. Mexico was a seat of culture and learning with a university, books, and printing presses half a century before the first bedraggled shiploads of Englishmen built their shabby huts at Jamestown. A poor lot this vanguard of the First Families of Virginia was, sweepings of debtors' prisons, runaway apprentices, ne'er-do-wells calling themselves gentlemen for want of a better term on the ship manifests, so poor that half of them died during the first year from fever, Indian tomahawks, and ennui.

What was that Western Ocean that King James named as the western boundary of his first colony? The Spaniards could have told him, but English and Spanish were not exactly on speaking terms. Only twenty years before Jamestown was founded, English ships had fought the Great Armada the length of the English Channel and sent the survivors limping home around the north of Scotland. To the first comers of

English blood there had to be a western ocean and not far away, over that hill or up that river — any river, Hudson, Potomac, James, Rappahannock. The early illusion that this new continent was only a brief interruption of a voyage to the wealth of the East was a long time dying. If anyone had told those first Americans that there were three thousand weary miles between Atlantic and Pacific shores they would have hooted in derision or made haste back to crowded England. Not knowing, they didn't run; the bliss of ignorance is illusory, but there are times when ignorance of the hazard may be helpful. By the time they knew the amazing truth they had the courage to look it in the eye.

The long process of poking into the wilderness that lay to the westward of the first colonies began early. At the start it was slow, venturing out from Boston to Concord, to Worcester, to the Berkshires, perhaps a mile a year on the average, a hundred miles in a hundred years, not exactly blinding speed. After English Wolfe beat French Montcalm at Quebec and took all Canada, the English wanted time to look things over and add up the value of their considerable winning. So they drew a line along the crest of the Allegheny Mountains, known in colonial history as the Proclamation Line, and proclaimed this the temporary western boundary of the British colonies in North America. Beyond this there was to be no more settling or trading with the Indians or roaming through the woods to see what could be seen. In the meantime the Ohio River was to be the southern boundary of Quebec. The Secretary of State for the Colonies promised that there would be arrangements for licensing both settlers and traders as soon as he could get around to it. Then a new Secretary took over and promptly forgot his predecessor's promise. The colonials were not so absentminded and added the Proclamation Line and the Quebec Act to their growing list of grievances.

The people in western Pennsylvania had a more direct way
of dealing with this British expedient· They wasted no time
drawing lines on maps. They had no maps, but the men along
that frontier had stout hearts and sturdy legs and they kept
slipping across the line that the English had drawn, building cabins, trading with the Indians, hunting, trapping, roaming the woods. These men were of the generation of Daniel
Boone, Simon Kenton, Girty the Renegade, who liked red
skins better than white, George Rogers Clark. Before the Revolution was over Boone had guided groups of landlookers
through Cumberland Gap, named for the duke who crushed
Stuart hopes at the battle of Culloden. The Gap was in the
southwestern corner of Virginia along the Wilderness Trail
that Boone blazed to fall in love with the beautiful fertile
country of the Blue Grass, with its swarming herds of game,
buffalo, deer, and elk. Farther south men from North Carolina,
Scotch-Irish mostly, Robertson, MacDonald, Henderson, and
"Nollichucky Jack" Sevier, who was fated to meet Andrew
Jackson, another Scotch-Irishman, in a duel. These and others
were creating the republic of Franklin, later to be the state of
Tennessee.

It was a long time before tidewater Virginians took
thought of the region beyond the barrier of the Blue Ridge.
Early reports praised the beauty of the Shenandoah Valley and
the fertility of the soil as shown by the lush growth of grass,
but the Wilderness Trail that ran the length of the valley was
a highway for fast moving bands of young Iroquois braves
looking for Creek or Cherokee scalps in the south. The early
settlers along the Shenandoah were mostly Scotch and Germans
from Pennsylvania mistakenly called "Dutch." They were
stolid, hard working farmers who cleared their fields, built
their cabins, and gathered large families about them.

In 1716 came the most bizarre company of explorers in all our history. The "Knights of the Golden Horseshoe" were a gallant company of brilliantly arrayed riders from the tide-water estates, led by Governor Spotswood playing hooky from his palace in Williamsburg. The horses of the cavalcade rivaled their riders in proud regalia of silver-mounted saddles and bridles. To each Knight was given a golden horseshoe bearing a motto in Latin, *Sic jurat transcendere montes* (Thus he swears to cross the mountains). This throwback to the days of King Arthur was no doubt edifying to the handful of ragged Indians and placid German farmers who may have seen them. At least it illustrated the distance that Virginians had come from the starving time that the first comers had known. The mountains would be transcended, but not by lords and ladies in holiday attire. The Knights glittered for a moment in the mountain sunshine and then faded back to their tobacco fields.

The new United States had been a large landowner from the beginning, in reality since 1609 when the second charter of the colony of Virginia had declared all the land "west and northwest" of Virginia as far as the "Western Ocean" to be the property of the poverty-stricken colony at Jamestown. This was the act of bandy-legged, sandy-haired Scotch Jamie, James I of England, James VI of Scotland, son of Mary of Scotland and the Isles. Proof of royal generosity? Not one of his sandy hairs was generous. Merely an indication of royal ignorance. He had never seen this distant colony of his and never would see it. Why not give it to his friends the Merchant Adventurers sitting comfortably in London who were equally ignorant? It cost him nothing and it might help in their search for gold and the Northwest Passage. Of course they found neither gold nor the way to the western ocean.

The westward movement that has been in slow progress ever since the founding of Boston accelerated after the Revolu-

tion and by 1800 had reached the Mississippi. To the early comers this great river served as the Western Ocean of the second
charter of Virginia. Here was a barrier beyond which stretched
an unknown wilderness inhabited only by wild beasts and wild-
er Indians. Now the human tide that had flowed steadily west
and northwest turned south heading down river for the markets and the overseas shipping at New Orleans. The western
bank of the river was Spanish territory, or so the settlers
thought. Navigable rivers are not good barriers or boundaries.
To the newcomers the Mississippi was a highway for trade and
boats and rafts appeared. The new settlements on the Ohio and
the upper Mississippi had furs, timber, pork, whiskey, barrel
staves, and hoop poles to trade to the Spanish. Let the Spanish
hold the western wilderness, soon to be named Iowa, Missouri,
Arkansas, if they liked. The new Americans would follow
the highways of trade. Sometimes the voyagers poled their
flatboats upstream against the current, but there was a good
market for the boats in Natchez and New Orleans and soon
the homeward bound rivermen had worn an overland trail
from Natchez to the Ohio which enjoyed a brief and sometimes
bloody history as the Natchez Trace.

Only at Natchez and New Orleans and upriver at St.
Louis did the French and Spanish show signs of anything like
solid communities along this river highway. At the end of the
Seven Years' War France had ceded her Louisiana domain to
Spain to keep it out of the hands of the British. Napoleon
cast envious eyes on this overseas empire and in 1801 made a
secret treaty with Spain at San Ildefonso by which title passed
back to France, Napoleon agreeing to make a Spanish prince
King of the Two Sicilies, a treaty that the dictator of Europe
never kept. That was the situation when Jefferson became
president in the spring of 1801. With a French governor in
residence and French uniforms on display the secret treaty

of San Ildefonso ceased to be very secret and the French further made their presence felt by clamping down on the river
trade.

The wharfage and storage space that had been granted
freely by the easy-going Spanish was now hedged about by re-
strictions and charges by the French. There were murmurs of
forcible action to keep the river open. That was the time of
Aaron Burr and Blennerhasset and the double-dealing Wilkin-
son. Why not an independent republic at the mouth of the
great river? There was even talk of war, but an easier way appeared.

The buying of Louisiana was by no means the first sign
of Jefferson's interest in the Northwest. As vice-president of
the Philosophical Society newly organized in Philadelphia he
had taken geography and exploration as his special province
and had attempted to raise money to send Andre Michaux,
botanist and explorer, to have a look at the mountains and
the country beyond. Michaux's estimate of the aid necessary
was absurdly small, but the amount raised was even smaller,
$128.25, and the Michaux plan withered on the vine. Then
while he was minister to France in 1786 Jefferson had a call
from a wandering American, one John Ledyard, who had a
wild-eyed proposal for exploration that appealed to the Jef-
fersonian imagination, nothing less than an approach to the
American Northwest by way of St. Petersburg and Siberia.
Jefferson contributed the logical suggestion that the wanderer
continue eastward over the Rockies and so find the westward
way to the Pacific Ocean by traveling east.

Ledyard was a Connecticut Yankee who had sailed with
Captain Cook and seen something of the northwest coast . Jefferson gave him letters to Russian officials who he hoped
would help this vagrant American on his way. The Empress of
all the Russians refused to listen to such an invasion of her do-

main but Ledyard set out across Siberia alone and without official sanction. He was within two hundred miles of Kamchatka and the Pacific when the Russians overtook him and hauled him back to the Polish border and shoved him across with orders to keep right on going. The "mad, romantic, dreaming Ledyard" came to the end of his earthly explorations when fever overtook him in Cairo still planning other adventures.

When Jefferson moved into the White House in 1801 his interest in exploration was greater than ever and now he might be able to do something about it; but something happened that surprised even this many-sided president. As has been told the Spanish authorities in New Orleans had been lax in the enforcement of such controls as they pretended to hold on trade down the Mississippi. Now by one of the mysterious shifts in Napoleonic policy French officials appeared in New Orleans and the old easy process of trading down river and storing goods in New Orleans to await shipment overseas was out. The river men must pay for what they got; even then they were lucky if they got it. Jefferson sent commissioners to Paris to bargain for enough territory at the mouth of the Mississippi to give the traders elbow room.

What happened then must have strengthened Jefferson's faith in destiny. Napoleon needed money to mount his oft-threatened invasion of England and offered the commissioners "the whole of Louisiana as received by us from Spain." It was the biggest real estate deal in history, an empire from the Mississippi to the Continental Divide for a price of fifteen million dollars, a bagatelle. Only eleven and a quarter million was actually for the land; the balance was for the payment of claims made by American merchants and shipowners against French privateers, most of which were never proved.

Of course there was opposition and criticism. Jefferson admitted that he "stretched executive authority until it cracked" and George Canning, head of the British Foreign Office, denounced the purchase as "receiving stolen goods from the greatest highwayman of the age." Obviously there was no constitutional warrant for such an act by the president — or anyone else — and Jefferson meditated asking for special legislation to authorize the step — after it had been taken — but was dissuaded from making what would have amounted to an admission of illegal action. The treaty with Napoleon was ratified by the Senate, the gold that Napoleon demanded was borrowed from a London banking house, and the United States was nearly doubled in size by the stroke of a pen.

CHAPTER II

Lewis and Clark

NOW THAT Jefferson had bought this vast domain what did it contain except deserts, mountains, buffalo, and savage Indians? A plan had been in the works before the agreement with France was settled. In 1803 Jefferson had commissioned Meriwether Lewis, once his secretary, and William Clark, younger brother of George Rogers Clark, the hero of Vincennes, to lead an expedition through the mountains to find a way to the Pacific Coast. The president's plans were modest and limited, apparently a combination of the commercial and scientific: find a route and bring back information on the topography and resources of the region. To these a political complexion was added by the purchase of the Louisiana Territory. Now this Northwest country was American, at least as far as the Continental Divide.

The Congressional appropriation was only $2,500. To save money soldiers, men already in government service, were assigned to the party. Both leaders had had experience as officers in Anthony Wayne's campaign against the Shawnees so it was natural for them to organize the expedition as a military unit. There were two captains, four sergeants, three interpreters, twenty-two privates, and nine or ten French-Canadians for boatmen and guides. Discipline was strict and trials were by court martial. A common punishment was fifty lashes on the bare back well laid on. John Collins was convicted of drunkenness on duty and for him the prescription was a hundred of the same. Collins' offense was aggravated by the fact that an important part of his duty was to guard the outfit's supply of whiskey which he had done by drinking it. One of the sergeants, a man named Floyd, died of fever during a conference with the Indians at Council Bluffs and was buried with military honors on a high bluff near by, afterwards called Floyd's Bluff. This was the only fatality on the long journey. The place where the council with the Indians was held was christened Council Bluffs and the name stuck.

The President's instructions to Meriwether Lewis, dated June 10, 1803, were much more limited than his large hopes: "The object of your mission is to explore the Missouri and such principal stream of it, as by its course and communication with the waters of the Pacific Ocean, may offer the most direct and practicable water communication across this continent for the purposes of commerce." A water route from ocean to ocean was an old dream that the president still cherished. To Lewis, Maria's River, which he named for his cousin Maria Wood, was to be an important link in this overland voyage. At the headwaters of this small stream one of the privates, a man named McNeal, stood with a foot on each side of the tiny trickle, a Rocky Mountain Colossus of Rhodes. Although he had chosen the river's name Lewis didn't think that the river measured up to the name, noting in his journal: "The hue of the waters of this turbulent and troubled stream did ill comport with the pure celestial virtue and amiable qualifications of that lovely fair one." It was so that polite young men of that day spoke of charming young ladies.

At the Mandan villages on the way up river the American captains were surprised to meet a "pedlar" (agent) from the Northwest Fur Company who gave the plausible explanation that he was only shopping around for horses and buffalo hides. The Nor'westers had been prompt to seize the opportunity suggested by McKenzie's trip through the Canadian Rockies to the great Fraser River and so to the Pacific, thereby getting a long jump on their rivals the Hudson's Bay Company in exploiting the fur possibilities of the northwest.

The upper Missouri was known to a few venturesome searchers, but not well nor to many. Scouts for the Northwest Company knew it better than did any of the people on the American side of the line. Vague as was the knowledge of the eastern side of the divide it was encyclopedic compared with what was known of the western slope. Here was strange country without perceptible trails or rivers or ranges as landmarks. Here they were on their own to find their way and make their maps and record their distances and directions. Fortunately both Lewis and Clark had had much experience in wilderness travel and were not easily bewildered.

Of the two Lewis was the better educated. He was a competent botanist and was able to identify and classify the strange plants of the prairie and mountains. He could also take observations to determine latitude and longitude. He had some slight knowledge of medicine and was the nearest approach to a surgeon the party could boast. One Whitehouse drank too much cold water when he was hot and tired in the long portage around the Falls of the Missouri and Lewis recorded that he "bled him plentifully from which he felt great relief. I had no other instrument with which to perform this operation but my penknife, however it answered very well."

A case of experimental therapy was the cure of a private, William Bratton (sometimes written Bratten or Brattin). This man became seriously ill with lumbago and was unable to regain his strength. As a last resort Lewis decided to test the virtues of the Indian sweat bath. The details were duly recorded in the official journal of the trip: "A hole about four feet deep and three in diameter was dug in the earth, and heated well by a large fire in the bottom of it. The fire was then taken out and an arch was formed over the hole by means of willow poles covered by blankets so as to make a perfect awning. The patient being stripped naked, was seated on a bench, with a piece of board for his feet, and with a jug of water sprinkled the sides and bottom of the hole, so as to keep up as hot a steam as he could bear. After remaining twenty minutes in this situation, he was taken out, immediately plunged twice in cold water, and brought back to the hole, where he resumed the vapor bath. During all this time he drank copiously a strong infusion of horse mint, which was used as a substitute for seneca root. At the end of three-quarters of an hour he was again withdrawn from the hole, carefully wrapped, and suffered to cool gradually." Heroic treatment but it worked and Bratton was soon back in active service.

Clark was less military than Lewis and consequently more concerned with the daily routine of the trail. His lack of formal schooling was revealed by the frequent phonetic guesses in his part of the official journal. Moccasin becomes "mockersin," mosquitoes are "musquetors," few is "fiew," fatigued is "fatiguad." In at least one instance gentle breeze is written "jentle brease." Lewis was subject to occasional periods of melancholy and depression while Clark was clearly enjoying every day, however hard. It was he who became a firm friend of the Indians, our first Commissioner of Indian Affairs in the new territory and the magnet which drew many chiefs and messengers to his Missouri home, while Lewis was to die alone in an empty house in Virginia in circumstances that strongly suggested suicide.

The supplies they carried with them were the standard army rations of that time with none of the condensed foods of to-day. For meat they must depend on the country through which they traveled and meat was basic. Their daily prayer might well have been "Give us this day our daily meat." Their stand-ard supply for a day, if they could get it, was four deer, or an elk and a deer, or one buffalo. Lewis recorded the menu for his supper for June 13, 1805: "My fare is really sumptuous this evening, buffalo hump, tongue, and marrow bones, fine trout, parched meal, pepper and salt, and a good appetite; the last is not considered the least of the luxuries." On many days breakfast was when they could shoot it. A common entry in the journal was: "Killed a doe and we halted and took break-fast."

Catching the meat for the day was sometimes a grim and dangerous business. On one occasion Lewis had narrow escapes from an indignant grizzly and two belligerent buffalo in close succession. Willing to call it a day he lay down under a tree to sleep it off, waking after an hour or two to find a large rattle-snake as near neighbor only ten feet away. No wonder he con-cluded that "all the beasts of the neighborhood had made a league to destroy me."

A member of the party who has received at least her full share of credit, if not more, is Sacagawea, "the Bird Woman." She was a Shoshone who had been carried off by the Minitarees and had finally, by a process of barter or capture, become the wife of a French-Canadian acting as guide and in-terpreter. She had little knowledge of Sioux or Blackfeet speech, but as she neared her Shoshone homeland she was of substantial service in smoothing the way for the travelers. To Lewis she was a servant, "If she has enough to eat and a few trinkets to wear I believe she would be perfectly content any-where." Clark, being less strictly military, called her "Janey" and her baby son born along the trail was "my little dancing boy Baptiest." He also called him Pompey and promised to provide for his education. The career of the young Pompey is obscured by legends and inventions. Trappers told stories at rendezvous campfires of someone called Charbonneau and since that was the name of the French-Canadian father many believed that here was the boy. Another yarn that seems wildly absurd was that the lad was educated at the court of a German prince, possibly Prince Paul of Wurtemberg, and later drifted back to his native mountains. The different versions had one thing in common, their improbability.

Communication with Sacagawea was a triple play process, Sacagawea in Shoshone to her husband, the latter in French to a mulatto from the French West Indies, who passed the message on to the heads of the party in broken English. It was slow and awkward but it worked surprisingly well.

The keepers of journals, there were several besides the two captains, recorded no trouble with the Indians, even with the dreaded Blackfeet, a security probably due to the military training and behavior of the men. There were no thrilling escapes from hostiles, no gallant rescues to record, only the humdrum routine of the march. To real explorers the best day is that on which there is little sensational to remember. Food was harder to find as they slogged through mountains and canyons on their way to the Columbia and so to the Western Ocean, twisting and turning to find their "practicable" route. The one they found was not the shortest or the easiest, but it was practicable as they proved by traveling it.

From the Pacific Lewis reported to Jefferson on results to that point, giving the total mileage from the mouth of the Missouri by stages: Missouri mouth to Great Falls, 2575; Great Falls to Kooskooske (Clearwater now), 340; Kooskooske and the Columbia to the mouth of the latter, 640. Total mileage,

3555. In that distance they had crossed the Continental Divide seven times in six different places; Lemhi Pass, Lolo Pass, Gibbon's Pass, Lewis and Clark Pass, Bozeman Pass, and a pass for which they had no name. It had been long and hard, but a way had been found from ocean to ocean. It would take forty more years to confirm it, but the Northwest was on its way into the Union.

Before tackling the high passes of the main range on their way home the explorers took time out to condition themselves for the stiff climbs ahead of them, setting up a program of foot races with Cayuse Indians in the Bitter Roots, with prisoner's base and quoit pitching for good measure. Perhaps as a result of these games the return trip was easy and uneventful as such trips go, but there was an individual variation that would have important results which would later become apparent. John Colter, a private, had fallen under the spell of the mountain country and as they neared the Mandan villages he asked for his discharge in order that he might turn back to the mountains and try his hand at trapping. He had been a good soldier and was known as competent and resourceful. Permission was granted promptly and he was provided with a good outfit. That was after talking with two hunters they had met the day before making their way up river. The place of Colter's departure was given as a point about fifty miles above the present city of Bismarck, the capital of North Dakota. The date was mid-August, 1806.

The account of the adventures of this lone wanderer as related by Colter to John Bradbury and recorded by the latter in his "Travels in North America" is the chief source of our information about him. He seems to have set out for St. Louis after his first winter in the mountains. Somewhere near the mouth of the Platte he met Manuel Lisa on his way upriver hoping to penetrate the rich beaver country of the Blackfeet. (Lisa was to be heard from often in the near future.) Colter was persuaded to turn back into the mountains as a guide for the Spanish trader. This was the beginning of a trip that rivaled the best that had been done before or was to be done in the future. The first stage was an errand to the Crows at Lisa's direction. His route is now fairly well known — over the Wind River Mountains and the Tetons into Pierre's Hole where he overtook the main body of the Crows with whom he fought in a long battle against the Blackfeet (possibly the Gros Ventres of the Prairie, often mistaken for the Blackfeet by early explorers). In spite of a wound in the leg incurred in that fight Colter then set out to reach the fort that Lisa had established somewhere to the northeast.

This was the stage on which he found himself in what is known now as Yellowstone Park. He noted the hot springs and the geysers but seems otherwise to have taken this part of his trip in his stride. Sticking to his remarkable sense of direction and distance he crossed the Park from southwest to northeast and reached Lisa's post in safety. This, had he known it, was the high point of his long wandering, although his report of geysers and hot springs and bubbling tar pits was long viewed as only an example of the typical tall tales of trappers and mountain tramps. The region received the name of Colter's Hell and no attempts were made for several years to confirm or disprove his absurd yarn.

Colter's immediate concern after rejoining Lisa was to continue his efforts on Lisa's behalf to make contact with the Blackfeet. In the course of his probings through the mountains, this time with a white companion, he was captured by Blackfeet who killed his partner and stripped Colter naked and set him on foot on the prairie with a lead of three or four hundred yards to run for his life. He escaped by diving into a river, possibly the Yellowstone, and hiding under a pile of

driftwood. After seven days he reached Lisa's fort on the Bighorn.

This was the end of Colter's extraordinary odyssey. In
the spring of 1810 he paddled alone in a small canoe for thirty
days down the Missouri to St. Louis, having come a distance
estimated by himself as three thousand miles.

Chittenden in his history of the fur trade concludes that
Colter's report of his experiences was entirely correct and enu-
merates his achievements: first to explore the valley of the Bighorn, first to cross the passes at the head of the Wind River
and see the headwaters of the Colorado; first to see the Tetons,
Jackson's Hole, Pierre's Hole and the sources of the Snake
River, and above all else the first to set eyes on the terrifying
wonders of the Yellowstone. Most of the time he traveled
through dangerous Indian country. Chittenden classed his exploits as "among the most celebrated performances in the
history of American exploration."

Chapter III

In the Reign of King Beaver

HARD ON the heels of the explorers, McKenzie in Canada and Lewis and Clark south of the border, came the trappers and traders. Neither knew much about latitudes and boundaries or cared although their leaders had a general idea of the division of territory. Early in the history of the French and British exploitation of the New World, particularly that part of it called Canada, the wealth of fur had been noted. There were furbearers well distributed over the continent, fox, seal, sea otter, fisher, marten, raccoon, deer, bear, beaver, buffalo, but beaver was the great staple and would continue to be so long as fashion decreed high bell-crowned beaver hats. All along the northwestern frontier beaver skins, "plews," were the chief circulating medium, accepted without question by buyers and sellers alike, and it was around beaver that a combination of profitable trade and a large chapter in the American saga develop. The westward movement that had been so slow in the early years and decades of our history now quickened from a crawl to a stride. Men knew now that there was a western ocean and began to make good guesses at the distance and the way there. Alexander McKenzie had made his way through the Canadian Rockies to the Fraser and down that turbulent stream and across to the Pacific. That was in 1792. Before that happened he had made his way in his search for beaver north to the river that bears his name flowing to the Arctic. Here was an empire to offset the loss of the American colonies in the Revolution a decade earlier. When Lewis and Clark matched KcKenzie's exploit on the American side of the border the stage was set for a drama that would fill the minds and hold the interest of men for nearly half a century.

The size of the stage on which this play was enacted was from the headwaters of the Missouri to the Pacific and south to the northern limits of the then Spanish colonies of New Mexico and California. Boundaries were uncertain. The nearest approach Napoleon could make to exactness was the euphemistic phrase "as received by us from Spain," a nice way of summing up the secret treaty with Spain that he never kept. Beyond the mountains there was a conflict of claims. Lewis and Clark claimed Oregon for the United States by right of discovery and exploration, but the Hudson's Bay Company was on the spot and for thirty years the only functioning government in the area that we now know as Washington and Oregon was that exercised by H.B.C. factors, especially by John McLoughlin. It should be noted that the factors were in the main just and tolerant, as American settlers in Oregon could testify, but helpful as they were to those in need of help they would brook no competition in their chosen field.

St. Louis was a natural center for trade with the tribes on the upper Missouri and the purchase of Louisiana was hardly completed when the keel boats began to head up the Missouri loaded with goods to catch the eyes of the Indians. A unique sort of triple play was required before the transfer of that part of the territory was validated, Spain to France and France to the United States, made necessary by the secrecy attendant on the French acquisition of Louisiana two years before the sale to

the United States. No other American city can boast of flying the flags of three different nations within the space of a
single day.

The first fur company to appear in the river metropolis
was the Missouri Fur Company, officially the St. Louis Missouri River Fur Company. It was under the headship of
Manuel Lisa and Lisa was the head of it in all ways. Born of
Spanish parents in New Orleans in 1772 he seems to have come
upriver to St. Louis as early as 1792. Chittenden reports that
the Spanish government granted him a monopoly of the fur
trade with the Osages about 1800, at which time he seems to
have been well established with credit. From that time until
his death in 1820 the history of the Missouri River fur trade
is the history of Manuel Lisa. He was a driving, magnetic
figure whose men followed him implicitly whatever the risk or
the hardship. He made at least twelve trips up the Missouri
and his total mileage on the river has been estimated at 26,000
miles and the time spent afloat perhaps three years in all. He
seems to have spent at least three winters in the wilderness. He
got on well with the Indians except the implacable Blackfeet
and for the twenty years that he ruled the river his posts domi-
nated the trade along the upper Missouri. Andrew Henry was
his ablest lieutenant in the establishment and operation of posts
in Indian country. In 1810 Henry was in the thick of a bloody
fight with the Blackfeet at the Three Forks of the Missouri, in
which the Indians had the upper hand. Henry then went over
the Divide and built a post on a branch of the Snake River,
becoming the first American trader to carry on his business
on the Pacific slope.

Even at that early date Lisa did not have his own way
entirely in the upper Missouri country. It will be recalled
that Lewis and Clark found an agent of the Northwest Company visiting with the Mandans and the Hudson's Bay Com-

pany was always to be expected. This company had been char-
tered by Charles II as a means of rewarding some of the noble
lords who had helped him to his seat on the British throne in
1660. The Governor and Company of Adventurers of England Trading into Hudson's Bay was ostensibly restricted to
the rivers flowing into the Bay, but the restriction was more
ostensible than real. This was a big country and there were
many rivers filled with beaver. The H.B.C. paid feudal dues
to the king of "two elks and two black beaver," to be paid
when his majesty visited Hudson's Bay.

The Northwest Company, later to be absorbed by the
powerful H.B.C., was almost feudal in concept and operation.
It was formed by a group of merchants in Montreal who wea-
ried of the cutthroat competition of free traders after the defeat of the French at Quebec. There were twenty-three partners or shareholders stationed at strategic points from Montreal
to the interior. Other partnerships might be earned by a seven-
year apprenticeship as clerks in the field, if voted by the unan-
imous approval of the partners already in, a prize not easily
won. In all there were over two thousand clerks, interpreters,
and voyageurs.

The Nor'westers were the aristocrats of the trade, each
partner regarding himself as the head of a savage domain in
which he ruled as lord of life and death. Each year all the
partners gathered at Fort William at Grand Portage on the
northwestern shore of Lake Superior. To this meeting the
partners came in state, especially those from Montreal, bringing
imported delicacies and vintage wines to grace the board. Then
there was feasting and drinking, dancing and carousing, sometimes fighting. But there was also work to be done, reviewing
the accomplishments of the year, analyzing the failures, deter-
mining policy for the year ahead, and plotting the action to be
taken against the hated H.B.C. A lesser company was the

Mackinaw Company which operated around the Great Lakes and along the upper Mississippi.

By 1810 the name of John Jacob Astor on the American side was well known among the overlords of fur. Born in Germany in 1763, the son of a peasant, he arrived in New York at the age of twenty. By 1810 his American Fur Company was one to be reckoned with and he was looking for a larger field than the local bits and pieces to be found along the Hudson River and in the Adirondacks. Already his impudent young clerks had nicknamed him "Old Man," "Old Cock," "Old Tyger."

There, then was the empire of beaver as it emerged from the findings of the explorers of the Northwest; anchored on the rivers flowing into the Bay was the Hudson's Bay Company (H.B.C., "Here Before Christ" in the speech of the irreverent trappers) and The Northwest Company from their headquarters at Fort William laying claim to the territory drained by the rivers flowing into the Mississippi, the Pacific, and the Arctic. Below the boundary the Missouri Company asserted an overlordship of the upper Missouri and was beginning to peer over the Divide, with the Astor company making threatening gestures that might be dangerous.

Astor alone among the contenders was familiar with European commerce and finance and knew the richness of the markets there from frequent visits and careful study. His active imagination led him to look farther to the possibility of a world-wide trade that included the Orient, especially China, and the wealthy buyers of Europe. He had considered the significance of Gray's voyage to the Northwest coast that had added the Columbia River to the list of great river highways. The sea otter alone was a bonanza for trade with the lordly Chinese mandarins. Why bother over petty bartering with Indians for their small catch when a headquarters post at the mouth of the Columbia would open the trade of the globe to enterprising Americans?

There was a political aspect of such a bold thrust into the northwest of which Astor was well aware. The British were already strongly based along the coast and the Russians to the north and the Spaniards in the south were eager to put a finger in the pie. The Spaniards could be ignored, but not the Russians; the distance from Alaskan ports to China was short and the Russians were beginning to increase their hold along the northwest coast. All this Astor made it his business to know and he was prompt to pass on his information to the powers that were in Washington. But Jefferson was no longer in the White House and Madison's mind was parochial, at least not international. Gallatin gave a friendly ear to the Astor urging, but Congress and the White House looked the other way. The government might close its eyes to the imperial possibilities of the northwest but not Astor.

His first move on the huge chessboard was the chartering of a ship from the U. S. Navy; the administration might not be willing to take a hand in the game but it was not above accepting the price of a charter from the lone player. The ship was the *Tonquin* and the captain was a man named Thorn, a naval officer and by navy standards a good one. The mission of the *Tonquin* was to take a cargo of men and material around Cape Horn to the mouth of the Columbia, there to build a stockade and begin trading with the Indians. This distant post, to be christened Astoria, was to be the northwest headquarters of the Astor commercial empire with the Orient as a port of call on the way to the markets of Europe.

The voyage of the *Tonquin* was a turbulent one. Captain Thorn was an able navigator but no part of a diplomat and the ship had hardly cleared Sandy Hook when trouble began. The passengers were traders and voyageurs going out to set up an important center of empire and they knew no master but Astor and Thorn was a navy martinet who recognized no authority on his quarter-deck higher than himself. That was the navy way and this was a navy ship. The first flareup came when the *Tonquin* called in at the Falklands for fresh water and such supplies as could be had there. The passengers saw a chance for a run on shore and a go at the flocks of wild ducks and geese that filled the air. Thorn looked askance at such frivolity and served notice that the ship would sail when sailing time came and any passengers not on board then would be marooned and might shoot to their heart's content. A head wind prevented Thorn from carrying out his threat, although there is evidence that one Robert Stuart threatened to spill the captain's brains on the deck if he didn't wait for the others. Stuart would be heard from again. The breach between the captain and the Astor men widened as the voyage continued. The traders had brought with them considerable quantities of goods of their own purchasing for providing some amelioration of the dull menus of the ship or for trading on their account after reaching their destination. Thorn regarded all articles in the cargo as ship stores to be used as he decided and refused permission to any but the ship's officers to touch the cargo, which did nothing to increase his popularity with the travelers.

There was more trouble at the mouth of the Columbia. At the best the entrance into the river guarded by a dangerous bar was a tricky one. There were no charts and boats were put out to find a way in. Thorn was dogmatic and stubborn and impatient of the delay. Boats were lost and eight men were drowned. After a site for the stockade had been found Thorn stormed over the time spent in building the post and took upon himself the selecting of the goods to be left there for the trading. He was under orders to proceed north to the sea otter country and do some trading on his own account.

The end of the *Tonquin* and her captain was a tragic one. Thorn rejected the advice of experienced men and permitted mobs of Indians to come aboard contrary to the customary procedure of dealing with a few at a time. Despising the chaffering in which the natives took delight Thorn resented the long bargaining chiefly by signs. Finally in a rage he struck one of the Indians and ordered him below in irons. The outcome of this major indiscretion was inevitable. Hordes of natives captured the ship and killed the captain and crew, burning the ship. The best that could be said for Captain Thorn was that he had landed men and material at the mouth of the Columbia and that trading had begun, but it was not an auspicious beginning.

Fortunately for the Astor plans this single voyage was the only one that was projected. The voyage around the Horn was too long and too hazardous for constant use and an overland link between New York and the Columbia must be forged if the New Yorker was to meet the competition of the Northwest Company moving out along the Canadian boundary. Wilson Price Hunt of New Jersey was chosen to head the company that Astor was sending out to find a good way through the mountains that would serve his purpose. Hunt's only experience in fur trading was the supplying of trade goods in St. Louis for the trip up the Missouri. On the surface Astor's reasons for the selection of Hunt are vague, but he knew the man and had confidence in his ability to organize and administer. These after all were the important considerations. Lesser men could do the trading and deal with the Indians, but for the man at the top a different and perhaps higher skill was necessary. That Astor was sure the man from New Jersey had.

Hunt's first task was to recruit the men for the overland trip through the mountains somewhere south of the route that Lewis and Clark had taken, if possible clear of imminent danger of Indian attack. The point from which to launch this hazardous enterprise was obvious. It was St. Louis, thence up the Missouri to the mountains. From there to the mouth of the Columbia where a stockade was presumably ready in operation they would be on their own with only such help as guides and guesses might offer. A good place to look for men was at Michilimackinac where the small Mackinaw Company had its headquarters. There were plenty of men there footloose and free, but they were mostly French-Canadians, gay and reckless and good canoemen, but only fair packers with little stomach for the long hard drag through the mountains to the Columbia. Hunt hit on a bizarre expedient to tempt these careless, vain children of the wilderness, the gift af a brightly colored cock's feather to wear in their hats. The sight of these "volunteers" strutting through the streets of Michilimackinac brought recruits in plenty, more than Hunt needed. He also added Donald McKenzie, a veteran of the trade and a good man with Indians. He had been with the Nor'westers, but the long climb to a partnership had filled him with disgust and he was ready for a new adventure. The arrangement with McKenzie did not seem a wise omen, a co-leadership that was bound to produce friction. Compared with McKenzie, Hunt was a rank amateur in the field and the ex-Nor'wester was not unwilling to let this be known. In reality the trouble that developed was of small importance and McKenzie more than paid his way. He was to become one of the more valuable men of the Astor organization.

The coming of the Hunt-McKenzie party was not welcome at St. Louis where Lisa ruled as lord of the upper Missouri country. Back of Lisa stood the Bents and the Sublettes and the other Missouri veterans. Washington Irving in "Astoria," the classic account of the trip to the Columbia, describes St. Louis as the invaders saw it on their arrival there, September 3, 1810:

"There were to be seen, about the river banks, the hectoring, extravagant, bragging boatmen of the Mississippi, with the gay, grimacing, singing, good-humored Canadian voyageurs. Vagrant Indians, of various tribes, loitered about the streets. Now and then a stark Kentucky hunter in leathern hunting dress, with rifle on shoulder and knife in belt, strode along. Here and there were new brick houses and shops set up by hustling, driving, and eager men of traffic of the Atlantic states, while on the other hand the old French mansions, with open casements, still retained the easy indolent air of the original colonists; and now and then the scraping of a fiddle, a strain of an ancient French song, or the sound of billiard balls, showed that the happy Gallic turn for gayety and amusement still lingered about the place."

The Astor men wasted little time studying the colorful scene along the streets and wharves. The time was September, winter would be upon them soon, and there was much to be done. It was a matter of course that Lisa would do what he could to block the newcomers, so it was necessary to get clear of St. Louis and Lisa's influence without delay. But the days passed too swiftly and there was much bickering and bargaining in the purchase of supplies. The thrifty Hunt, seeking to save money and at the same time handicap Lisa's plans, whatever they were, moved his men up the Missouri to a point near a small stream called the Nadowa (Nodaway) east of Kansas City, not far away from the future site of St. Joseph— destined to be the jumping-off place for both Santa Fe and Oregon bound parties. It was at the Nadowa that Robert McClellan was added to the outfit. This new recruit hated Lisa whom he charged with inciting the Indians to break McClellan's trade on the upper river. He swore to kill him on sight if he found him in the wilderness. Whatever the merit of his complaint McClellan was always a lone wolf whom other men would find it difficult to deal with. Ramsay Crooks, formerly a Nor'wester and now a partner of McClellan on the Missouri, sharing McClellan's distrust of the powerful Lisa, also joined Hunt at the Nadowa. These two men warned the man from New Jersey to watch his step with the Sioux and the Blackfeet, always uncertain tribes.

The Missouri was a highway of adventure and possible profit, drawing men of many diverse kinds. With Hunt there was Joseph Miller, former army officer, well educated, of good family, and experienced in the ways of Indians in beaver country. Hunt met him in St. Louis and promptly snapped him up as a partner. Even on the empty stretches of the upper river recruits appeared. Near the Sioux country the Hunt party met two independent trappers, Benjamin Jones and Alexander Carson, in a canoe bound down river for a spree after two years in the mountains. Hungry and thirsty for the delights of civilization as they must have been, at a word from Hunt these men turned back for the long grind through the mountains to the mouth of the Columbia.

One man who joined Hunt brought with him a special grievance. That was Pierre Dorion, a halfbreed who had been in Lisa's service as an interpreter and who broke with him over Lisa's charge of ten dollars a quart for whiskey provided him the previous year. He may not have known that whiskey of no worse quality was often sold on the upper Ohio for as little as twenty-five cents a gallon, but he knew that ten dollars a quart was too much. Dorion signed on with Hunt at an increase in pay, stipulating that his Indian wife and two children should accompany him. Lisa threatened to arrest him for debt and

Hunt determined to set out from the Nadowa before Lisa could act.

The Missourian was not so immersed in his quarrel with Dorion that his eyes were closed to his own upriver interests. It was time for him to bring down the winter's catch of fur and if possible pick up news of Andrew Henry in command of the post on the upper waters of the Snake. There was another reason for Lisa's desire to overtake Hunt; that was to confront the dangerous Sioux with the combined strength of the two parties. Even the Sioux would think twice before attacking so strong a force, so Lisa put on the pressure to overtake Hunt below the Sioux country. Hunt had a long start on him, nineteen days and two hundred miles, but Lisa had the best keelboat on the river and a picked crew of twenty men. Above all he had himself, tireless, gay, inspiring, and wise in the tricky ways of the Big Muddy.

The life of a boatman on the Missouri was not a merry one. First there was the current of the river, seldom over two miles an hour except in high water, but it was always there, relentlessly pushing the boats back. There was a single mast on a keelboat on which a sail could be rigged when the direction and force of the wind permitted, which wasn't often. The course of the Missouri resembled that of a broken backed snake and a fair wind sending them happily upward could suddenly become a head wind as the river swung around the unpredictable bends. Much of the propulsion was provided by using poles. Along the sides was a clear runway, walkway rather, from bow to stern. The crew lined up with poles in hand to set the pole firmly in the muddy bottom of the river and walk with it to the stern, literally walking the boat upriver.

The real test of the mettle of a crew was the cordelle. This was a long line attached to the top of the stubby mast. All hands except the bourgeois, the combined captain, trader, steersman, lined up on the cordelle and dragged the unwilling boat upstream by "main strength and awkwardness." The men, bent double with their effort, stumbled over drift logs, sank in the mud of the banks, fought their way through the tangle of bushes and briars that lined the river. An Indian attack at such a time could be disastrous to everyone except the Indians. A liberal pouring of rum or whiskey after a bout on the cordelle was small enough reward for such herculean effort.

If the weather had not seemed to conspire against him Lisa had reason to believe he could overtake the Hunt party before the Sioux country was reached, but storms and strong head winds held him back. When he reached the Omaha villages he was forced to send a messenger overland asking Hunt to wait for him and giving the reason for his request. The word reached Hunt at the mouth of the Niobrara and he pretended to agree, but McClellan and Ramsay Crooks distrusted Lisa and persuaded Hunt that the threat of Indian difficulty was only one of Lisa's tricks: so in spite of his promise to wait, Hunt pushed on upriver.

There in brief is the background of the most extraordinary event in the whole history of the trade, a race of eleven hundred miles lasting two months. Near the end of May the whimsical weather turned fair and when he learned the flimsy character of Hunt's promises Lisa really put on the pressure, more than once traveling nearly all night and once covering seventy-five miles in twenty-four hours, a keelboat record for the river. Lisa and Hunt both talked their way past hostile Indians. The race ended on June 2 when Lisa overtook the Hunt party and they stopped for a parley. Lisa renewed his demand on Dorion and serious trouble was averted only by the intervention of cooler heads. The two parties traveled together as far as the Aricara villages just above the mouth of the Grand River — thirteen hundred and twenty miles from the mouth of the Missouri. Lisa and his tireless men had averaged more than eighteen miles a day for sixty days, a superhuman feat. It should be added, to complete the record, that when Lisa appeared McClellan conveniently forgot his threats of violent reprisal.

Lisa was near the end of his trip but Hunt and his men had still to cross the mountains to find a way, or make one, down the Columbia to its mouth where they hoped a stockade was being built to be the focus of the overseas trade. After parting with Lisa, Hunt decided to abandon his boats and take to horses, thus bypassing the dangerous Blackfeet. The Aricaras and Cheyennes on this part of the river were shrewd horse traders — and also clever horse stealers. Hunt's standard price per horse was ten dollars, payable of course in goods at "first cost." The first cost was determined by the white man and represented a large markup over the actual cost, a regular practice on the upper Missouri.

In the trade with the Indians all the advantages lay with the trader. He brought the goods, fixed the price, named the first cost, and ran the show generally. By way of example Machinaw muskets made in England, were popular with Indians and in steady demand. The cost in England was eight dollars per gun, in the trading post thirty dollars to the Indian. In the case of whiskey there was a double deal. What passed for whiskey was low grade alcohol liberally diluted with Missouri River water. To crown it all the trader determined the quality of the fur the Indian offered. A prime object always was to keep the trapper, Indian or white, in debt to the trader.

The Crows were the best bargainers in the mountain country, but the Aricaras were no amateurs. Hunt needed horses and he wanted them quickly and it is possible that this time the Indian had none the worst of it.

After a month of trading and reorganizing Hunt found himself at the head of sixty-four men and eighty-two horses, of which seventy-six carried packs filled with merchandise and equipment intended for Astoria. They were approximately two-thirds of the way from St. Louis to the mouth of the Columbia, but their real troubles were still ahead of them. The earlier stages had been comparatively simple although the leaders seemed uncertain as to the route and there was much doubling and twisting. Their general direction was westward and south-westward, skirting the Bighorn range and crossing the Wind River Mountains into the valley of the Green; then over Teton Pass to the Snake River, where Andrew Henry had built a post for the Missouri River Fur Company, Lisa's outfit. The country traversed, especially the Wind River and Green River valleys, was to become well known among mountain men as a frequent location of the annual fur rendezvous to be estab-lished by William H. Ashley.

The unusually large size of the Hunt party was an index of the Astor plans, but it was also a handicap, particularly where grazing was poor. The sight of the Snake River set the men to clamoring for another change, from horses back to boats. Hunt foolishly yielded, boats were contrived, and the flotilla set forth. For a week the voyageurs rejoiced in the rapid progress, then the turbulent Snake showed its true char-acter. A boat was wrecked, a man drowned, and impossible rapids lay ahead. The horses had been left in the dubious hands of two Snake Indians. Food was scanty and winter was near. Hunt broke his company into smaller groups, some to scout down river for navigable water, one to go back in hope of find-ing the horses left with the two strange Indians, others to hunt or to try their hand at trapping. The merchandise intended for the post at Astoria was hidden in nine caches.

Food was a constant problem for mountain travelers, but while wild game lasted they lived well. Buffalo was the favorite, especially humps and tongues, and fat beaver tail was not to be scorned. At the higher levels big horn mutton was popular. Deer were plentiful and elk a useful substitute, though likely to be tough. Antelope meat was a last resort. Veterans gave a high rating to panther meat, but greenhorns called them cats and let it go at that. Bear meat was apt to be fat and greasy, but it could be eaten in a pinch. Bear hams and shoulders well smoked were good eating, better to the old hands than those derived from the Missouri razorbacks.

The Hunt party lived well in spite of their numbers until after they reached "that accursed mad river" the Snake and started on the eight hundred miles that separated them from their goal at Astoria. The supplies that had seemed so lavish east of the Divide soon dwindled to forty pounds of corn, twenty pounds of grease, and five pounds of portable soup for all hands with five and a quarter pounds of dried beef ("jerky") per man. The condensed, dehydrated foods of today were of course unknown to these men and Hunt had not bothered to learn the Indian art of making pemmican when meat was abundant. Days passed with starvation threatening. Occasional Indians bartered dried fish with them, and now and then a scrawny horse might be picked up. Enough dog meat to go around was a banquet.

The point where they had abandoned the boats was given the name of "Caldron Linn," sometimes "Devil's Scuttle Hole." From there the various parties made their way to Astoria as best they could. McKenzie, McClellan, and Read, wise in the ways of mountain travel, joined forces and reached Astoria January 18, 1812. Nearly a month later Hunt and the main body of the expedition arrived, three hundred and ninety days after leaving St. Louis. Hunt's estimate of the distance

covered was thirty-five hundred miles. As an indication of
their wandering course it should be noted that the distance by
rail today is only twenty-three hundred miles.

At Long Narrows on the Columbia Hunt met with an
example of the grapevine telegraph among the Indians. Two
of them gave a circumstantial account of the destruction of
the *Tonquin* and the killing of the captain and crew.

A route of sorts had been found through the mountains,
in places close to the final choice of South Pass, but the Snake
River was still a problem and Astor's demand for a safer, faster route to the mouth of the Columbia was still to be met.

CHAPTER IV

The Mountain Men

WHEN HUNT and his men came together in the
stockade at Astoria their task was only half accomplished. The route they had found through the mountains was
better than that of Lewis and Clark but it was still not good
enough. There must be a shorter and safer route if the Astoria
enterprise were to prosper. If there were not such a route then
the long agony of Hunt and his men along the Snake and Columbia was a waste of time and hunger. As soon as they had
restored their strength in the comfort of the stockade Hunt
set about planning the final test, a return trip to plot a course
that would spell final success or failure. As leader of this critical adventure Robert Stuart, a nephew of the head of a small
Astor post on the Okanagon, was chosen. Born in Scotland,
as were so many men in the trade, he had come to Montreal at
the age of twenty-two as a clerk with the Northwest Company. Now he was an Astor partner with two shares. As one
of the passengers on the ill-fated *Tonquin* he had shown something of the stuff that was in him by threatening to spill Captain Thorn's brains on his quarterdeck if he persisted in his
threat to maroon the laggards on shore.

Here was a Homeric figure largely ignored by the writers of sober history. He was young and without experience as mountaineer or horseman. In fact he had had his first horseback ride about three months before he set out to find the perfect route that Astor demanded. His lack of horsemanship was of little importance as the Crows, horse thieves par excellence, ran off their horses before they were fairly on their way and set them on foot from there to the Missouri. Bad as was the reputation of the Crows as horse thieves, Robert Campbell who knew them well had a good word for them: "Trust to their honor and you are safe; trust to their honesty and they will steal the hair off your head." Stuart's men were a discordant lot and hard to hold in line. Food was scanty until they reached buffalo country over the mountains. There were many opinions about the proper direction to take, but Stuart was tireless and intelligent and soon developed the trailmaker's instinct for divining a course from the contours of the land and the course of rivers. At that they were ten months on the way. Their first choice of a secure shelter for winter quarters was soon spotted by thieving Indians and they were forced to try again. As they neared the Missouri, rivermen told Stuart that the United States was at war with England, but that was no affair of his and he accomplished his purpose and delivered his message to Astor. His carefully kept journal shows that he covered 5,113 miles from Astoria to New York.

What Stuart had accomplished was of major importance, nothing less than the discovery of the elevated plateau of South Pass, soon to be the route of emigrants, Mormons, gold-hunters, and finally the first railroad to cross the main range of the Rockies. Compared with this stupendous feat the fact that the British had captured the stockade at Astoria and renamed it Fort George was an insignificant detail, whatever it may have been to Astor. That gentleman had known adversity and defeat before and had little respect for them. His dream of a world-wide trade starting at Astoria and ending in the rich markets of Europe was in the dust. Very well, he would make himself master of fur in the American northwest. Now that Lisa was dead and his tireless energy could not be duplicated Astor's American Fur Company was soon at the top. It had no friends and seemed not to feel the need of any.

Astor's men were ruthless and able. Kenneth McKenzie, former Nor'wester, born in Scotland of course, lived in almost regal state. To be invited to sit at his table in his headquarters post at Fort Union was like being presented at court. He had become an American citizen in 1822 and promptly organized the Columbia Fur Company for trade on the upper Missouri. As a competitor Astor found him unbeatable and was finally forced to come to terms with him or take a heavy loss. By the terms of agreement McKenzie and his partners became the Upper Missouri Outfit of the American Fur Company, virtually an independent organization. His attitude and power are indicated by the names given by trappers, "King of the Missouri," "Emperor McKenzie," "Emperor of the West."

He was a stern disciplinarian and a hard taskmaster. Told that Indians had attacked one of his parties and driven off the horses but that the men were safe, McKenzie lashed out, "Damn the men! If the horses had been saved it would have amounted to something." A constant irritation to him was the government's prohibition of the use of whiskey in trade with the Indians, a privilege which the Nor'westers and the H.B.C. enjoyed in Canada. Boats bound up river were stopped and searched at Leavenworth and any liquor found on board was confiscated. The prominence of the Astor company earned for their boats the special attention of the inspectors. McKenzie had what he thought was a legitimate idea, the building of a distillery near Fort Union, and one was actually operated for a short time as an alleged scientific experiment in the making of wine from native berries. The government wasn't having any of this and McKenzie lost his distillery. Smuggling was common and sometimes successful. In 1832 William Sublette secured a license to take in four hundred and fifty gallons of alcohol for his "boatmen," although he was traveling by horse power only.

Astor had many able men in the field, but none of them could equal McKenzie in ruthless, driving energy. Some of them were auras of mystery. James Archdale Hamilton was alleged to be an English nobleman in disguise. Lucian Fontenelle was suspected of having royal blood somewhere in his background; he was the one that the veterans viewed as the best leader of brigades or caravans and his parties always got through. His end was mysterious and tragic, suicide.

Pedigrees counted for nothing. If a man did his work well his name was what he said it was. The mountain wilderness took them in whatever they had been elsewhere and worked them over to its own likeness or killed them. In any case the mountains kept their secrets and respected their anonymity. Two of them left written records of their lives. Charles Larpenteur was one. His "Forty Years a Fur Trader on the Upper Missouri," was much used by Chittenden in his history of the fur trade. William Angus Ferris wrote a series of articles for the *Western Literary Messenger* under the title "Life in the Rocky Mountains." It was at least the testimony of an eyewitness and a participant. An agent for Astor among the Mandans was John F. A. Sanford who later gained a permanent place in American history by becoming the owner of Dred Scott whose suit for freedom did its bit toward bringing on the Civil War.

In the competition of the Astor company against the field there were two sets of ethics, one for the East, reliable, orderly, honest, and another for the West where traders like McKenzie barred no holds. Indians were encouraged to attack opposition traders; more than once there was strong suspicion of outright robbery and violence, and not by Indians only. It is idle to seek the primary responsibility for this state of affairs. The Hudson Bay Company with its monopoly on the Canadian side after its absorption of the Northwest Company could afford to be generous and hospitable to strangers, but on the American side the next casual visitor, however innocent seeming, might be a spy.

For all the organizing and administrative ability on the Astor team there were rival individuals and shifting groups who persisted and took their share of the profits. Some of these acquired prominence and a moderate profit as traders. An important point on the route from Missouri to Santa Fe was Bent's Fort on a branch of the Arkansas River, the Purgatoire, known to traders and trappers as the "Picketwire." Probably next to Laramie this was the strongest point west of the Missouri in those early days, a combination of trading post, fort, and gathering place for friendly Indians. Small cannon looked out through embrasures. Within the stockade were sleeping rooms, food, drink, even a billiard table, and safety. The Bents had Yankee blood and a Yankee sense of enterprise and adventure transmitted from Silas Bent their paternal grandfather who had been one of the leaders of the Boston "Tea Pary."

William H. Ashley of Missouri was scarcely a mountain man as were Jim Bridger (Old Gabe), the Sublettes, Kit Carson, Jedediah Smith the Bible reader, St. Vrain and a host of others, but he had access to capital and he had a sense of organization and administration that was uncommon in the trade outside the big companies. To him goes the credit for establishing a regular route to Oregon somewhere about 1824, perhaps earlier. For a number of years the point west of Independence where the Oregon emigrants branched off was marked by a sign bearing the simple legend "Road to Oregon." Seldom have three words conveyed so much fateful information to so many people.

For Ashley the fur trade was only a means for the rapid accumulation of the fortune that would set him up in politics, the career for which he yearned. He stayed in the trade only four years and made only a few trips to the mountains, chiefly to oversee the fur rendezvous for which he was responsible. Then he sold out to a triumvirate consisting of William Sublette, Jackson, and Jedediah Smith and with the fortune he needed turned back to politics. In his own way he was as much of a driver as was McKenzie for Astor. Both men knew what they wanted and went after it. In its issue of March 20, 1822, the *Missouri Republican* contained this challenge:

> To Enterprising Young Men:
>   The subscriber wishes to engage a hundred young men to ascend the Missouri River to its source, there to be employed for one, two, or three years. For particulars enquire of Major Andrew Henry, near the lead mines in the county of Washington, who will ascend with and command the party; or of the subscriber near St. Louis.
>
> William H. Ashley

Here are the names of some of the "enterprising young men" who took up the challenge: James Bridger, aged 18, Jedediah Smith, 25, Thomas Fitzpatrick, 24, who was to bear the name of "Broken Hand" and to spend thirty-one years on the frontier. William L. Sublette was to become one of the famous ones, a leader among independent traders and an explorer on his own account; James Clymer who kept a diary which did not see the light of print until 1928 was among them. Clymer's diary was scanty and curt and he did the elaborating in his own hand when the end of his life was near, doing much of this work on a child's slate because of failing eyesight. Clymer's spelling was decidedly free hand, but his reputation for truthtelling was of the best.

These men were of the company of trapper-explorers who wrote their names indelibly on the map of the Northwest, but it was Ashley who had the vision and the energy to make their dreams come true. By 1826, only four years after his modest announcement, he had accumulated a fortune in the fur trade and his men had covered the area of northern Colorado and Wyoming, much of Idaho, Nevada, and northern Utah. In one year Ashley parties had traveled from 40° north to the Columbia River at 47° 30'. In the rendezvous of 1825 on the Green River (Siskadee) Ashley and Smith-Sublette parties numbered a hundred and twenty men, some of them in the wilderness since 1822. By that time Smith had been north as far as the H.B.C. post at Flathead House, Sublette to the Bear River, and Bridger could tell of salt water which he thought might be the Pacific Ocean. It was really Great Salt Lake, first named Buenaventura and believed to empty into the Pacific a long seven hundred miles away over the high Sierras. Etienne Provost had gone down the Bear River and was perhaps the first man to see the great lake, three men found the lake within three months. Provost was to give his name to Provo now the seat of Brigham Young University.

The golden age of the trapper and trader began about 1810 and thirty years later it was nearing its end. What did it amount to to justify a place in an account of this Northwest that Lewis and Clark had revealed in their report? Few men were directly involved in it, perhaps five hundred in the mountain area on the average. The margin of profit demanded by the trader on goods sold to Indians and whites alike was fantastic. Lisa's charge of ten dollars a quart for whiskey furnished to Dorion was typical, although perhaps extreme. Whatever profit there was found its way into the pockets of a few men.

The men who risked their lives in that wild country took little and many lost their lives, possibly five hundred or more. A few facts remain although statistics of trapper casualties are generally vague and unreliable. In the space of two years the Missouri Company lost thirty-four men and fifteen thousand dollars worth of goods in fights with Blackfeet and Aricaras. In 1823 an Ashley party lost twenty-six men in battle with the Aricaras. Wyeth is reported as having taken two hundred men into fur country; three years later only forty were still alive.

For the operators at the top the margin of profit was large in the good years, estimated at seventy to eighty per cent as compared with a margin of twenty per cent in the trade with Santa Fe. In 1847 an Indian agent in St. Louis, Jim Dougherty, estimated the annual value of the fur trade at that river entry port at between two and three hundred thousand dollars. Such men as Pierre Chouteau, Jr., William H. Ashley, William Sublette prospered, the others lived from season to season.

It was not in annual profit that the fur trade justified its place in our history. The hunters of beaver were few in number, but they covered a wide territory, from the disputed Canadian boundary to the vague limits of Mexican territory in the southwest. They blazed trails and reported lakes and mountain passes. Usually mapmakers claimed most of the credit for those far wanderers were not cartographers. Some of them left their names on the land they traveled. Jackson's Hole, now a southern extension of Yellowstone Park, once a hideout for wanted men, probably owes its name to David E. Jackson of the Smith-Jackson-Sublette partnership that later acquired the Ashley interests in the trade. Pierre's Hole on the western side of the Tetons was named for an otherwise forgotten trapper, "Old Pierre" Tivanitagon. The city of Ogden, now second in size in the Mormon commonwealth, is a reminder of Peter Skene Ogden, chief trader for the H.B.C. in the Oregon country. Then there is the Henry River, a branch of the Snake and a monument to the Andrew Henry who was a pioneer trader for Manuel Lisa, and John Day's River, a tributary of the Columbia, named for one of the men who starved with Hunt on the slow drag down the Snake and the Columbia to the stockade at Astoria.

Many of the trappers could neither read nor write. Kit Carson spoke English, Spanish, and the language of half a dozen Indian tribes but he could not write his own name until his Spanish wife taught him. His last words were Spanish, "Adios, compadre." Before Captain Bonneville was credited with the "discovery" of the Great Salt Lake basin half a dozen trappers had seen the lake and set their traps in the fresh water streams flowing through the defiles of the Wasatch. Jedediah Smith, trapper, trader, and articulate reporter of things seen and done, found his way over the Mojave Desert and probably wound down Cajon Canyon to the San Gabriel Valley and nearly to San Diego. A second trip took him from near Los Angeles pueblo north to San Francisco and out over the high Sierras. He found fertile soil and friendly climate but no gold. That was left for other wanderers who failed to see the beauties that Smith praised.

Smith's trip over the Sierras was an ordeal. With two companions, seven horses, and two mules he made his way north of Yosemite, which he may have glimpsed, over the mountains, eight days in the mountain crossing and then twenty days on the desert to Great Salt Lake. His report of that ordeal was laconic: "When we arrived at the Salt Lake, we had but one horse and one mule remaining which were so feeble and so poor that they could scarce carry the little camp equipment which I had along; the balance of my horses I was compelled to eat as they gave out." Such privations were all in the day's work for the mountain men. Seven years later he took a flyer in the Santa Fe trade and died on the Cimarron with a Comanche lance in his back.   In three years west of the Rockies Smith covered eleven degrees of longitude and fourteen degrees of latitude stretching from Salt Lake to Monterey and from San Diego to the Columbia.   He was only thirty-three when the Comanches caught up with him on the Cimarron.

Not all the mountain men were heroic figures. The wilderness beckoned to individuals who had worn out their welcome elsewhere. Such a one was Mike Fink, known as a hard drinker along the Ohio and a devil among the women in a place and time when most rivermen were skilled in such arts. Mike appeared in the Indian country with two partners, Carpenter and Talbot. He and Carpenter had a showy exhibit which they usually put on when they were rather more than half seas over, taking turns shooting a tin cup filled with whiskey from the other's head at seventy yards.   Unfortunately they quarreled over a desirable squaw and chose their weird duello as a way of settling their rivalry. This time the bullet found the middle of Carpenter's forehead. Mike claimed accident but he had about reached the end of his string.   One day when he was more than usually drunk he boasted of shooting Carpenter and Talbot killed him where he stood.   Mike received better treatment than he deserved in John G. Neihardt's "Song of Three Friends."

Alexander Harvey was a shady character with the American Fur Company at Fort McKenzie. As the tale runs an Indian had killed a cow belonging to the post. Harvey caught the Indian redhanded and broke his thigh with a shot through the leg. Then Harvey filled his pipe and sat smoking as he delivered this exhortation: "Look well for the last time at all these nice hills — at all those paths which lead to the fort, where you come with your parents to trade, playing with your sweethearts —

look at that, will you, for the last time." Then knocking the ashes from his pipe he killed the offender. If anyone but the careful Chittenden had told this tale it would have been classed as at least semifictional.

Edward Rose and James Beckwourth were members of the Crow tribe. Rose, who was rumored to have been a pirate on the Mississippi, served as an interpreter for Hunt and in spite of a dubious reputation apparently gave loyal service. His mother was mixed Cherokee and Negro. Beckwourth wrote an autobiography while in the employ of the American Fur Company. His reputation was that of a "charming liar."

A feature of life in the mountains that always surprised the tenderfoot was the speed and extent of communication over that vast area, but the manner of it was no mystery. The annual rendezvous was an opportunity for gossip as well as trading, gambling and drinking. Men gathered in with their winter's catch of fur from great distances meeting old friends and companions and exchanging news of men and events. The fact that they were few in number added to the ease with which news traveled. One white man even in a range of hundreds of miles could hardly be overlooked. Where was he last seen? With whom was he working? Questions like these were passed around the camp fires at night. Crowded city streets gave better cover to hunted men than did the mountain wilderness. Of course there was loud boasting of deadly struggles with Blackfeet or Aricaras, Sioux or Shoshones. A hardy perennial was the tale of a petrified forest where petrified birds sang petrified songs.

A good example of these campfire narratives was the story of Old Hugh Glass. All that is known of his life before he arrived in the mountains is that he was born somewhere in Pennsylvania, date unknown. It is known that he was a member of Ashley's and Henry's party in 1823 and was wounded in a fight with the Aricaras that year. He was already called "Old Hugh," not necessarily a proof of age. He was with Andrew Henry in the latter's expedition to the Yellowstone River and served as a hunter. There are several versions of this part of the story or legend as it was told and retold with the inevitable embroidery around many campfires, but the main circumstances were fairly well authenticated. In thick underbrush he ran on a grizzly with cubs and wounded but failed to kill her with the one shot he was able to throw at her. Before his companions could come up he was so badly mauled and bitten that he was not expected to live. Henry hardly dared risk the failure of his trip up the Yellowstone by waiting in faint hope of Hugh's recovery and paid two men to stand by until he died. After a wait of five days these two characters, correct names unknown, gave up hope of a favorable outcome, left the supposedly dying man to his fate and took off to overtake the main party to report that Glass had died and that they had given him proper burial.

Instead of dying as expected Old Hugh survived and after a grueling trip of a hundred miles, crawling on hands and knees for long stretches, the tough old man reached Fort Kiowa on the Missouri near the present site of Chamberlain, South Dakota. There after only a few days' rest he joined a keelboat bound for the Yellowstone. But his troubles were not over. Not far from Tilton's Fort on the Missouri he took a short cut overland to stretch his legs, a fortunate thing for him as the boat was captured by the Aricaras and all the members of the crew massacred as they crept around the long bend. Glass was saved by Mandan warriors who carried him the rest of the way to the post, a Columbia Fur Company outpost. Without waiting for rest Glass set out that night to overtake Henry. After traveling for thirty-eight days alone through savage country he reached Henry who had established a fort near the Little Bighorn.

There were more hairline escapes for the old man, in the valleys of the Powder and the Platte, encountering his old enemies, the Aricaras. At Fort Atkinson he found one of his faithless companions who had left him to die alone and for some reason failed to take the revenge he had earned. The story of Old Hugh came to its end in the winter of 1832-33 when he was killed, "rubbed out" in the speech of the mountain men, by the Aricaras. It is only fair to say that many mountain men were skeptical of much of the Glass legend.

Nearly a hundred years later John Neihardt selected Old Hugh as the heroic symbol of the hard fighting, long enduring mountain man in an epic poem "The Song of Hugh Glass." In this the poet gives names to the faithless guards who had agreed to stand by Glass until he died, as expected, or recovered sufficiently to travel. They were a boy called Jamie and a French-Canadian Jules le Bon, both apparently fictional characters.

The mountains drew many men who were little fitted for the life of the trapper. There was Nathaniel Wyeth who had been a farmer near Cambridge, in Massachusetts. His first trading venture was far removed from trapping beaver, nothing less than selling ice in the West Indies, cutting the ice in Fresh Pond which is still there. He was a good salesman and he prospered. Looking about for another world to conquer he discovered the fur trade, but not as Carson and Bridger knew it. He would solve the problem of transportation with something that was faster and more flexible than the cordelle or the packhorse and came up with a combination of wagon and boat, probably the first amphibious craft in history. Unfortunately it didn't work, though Wyeth with true Yankee stubbornness lasted longer than any of the veterans believed possible, long enough to lose his own slender capital and that of his friends. He also caught a beaver in a trap of his own setting and duly recorded it. McKenzie said of him: "He is a man of many schemes and considerable talent."

A weird by-product of the time was Hale Jackson Kelley of Vermont who may have given Wyeth his initial interest in beaver. Kelley was an Oregon enthusiast at long range, long before he had a glimpse of that country. Here was an "earthly paradise" he declared and started his Oregon Colonization Society to promote emigration to the land of honey and hope. Near the end of his life he actually reached the Columbia by a long hard trip through northern Mexico to San Diego and up the California coast. He left no record of his impressions.

Captain Bonneville is one of the characters who is not easy to place, in spite of Washington Irving's valiant effort to present him as one of the important figures on the stage. He was of French descent, a graduate of the United States Military Academy and a captain in the regular service. The reports of adventure in the wilderness of the Rockies developed in him a dream of joining in the game. His was a double dream, to see the country wild and untamed and to pay his way by trapping on the side. This combination of romance and profit was not to be accomplished. Only those men with a single purpose could stand the gaff in that merciless land. Bonneville went many places, saw many things, including Indians and traders, but he was not trained as an explorer and he was too diffuse in his interests to match wits with the wily beaver.

Irving does his best with the captain, including the rather dubious report of a side trip into California as far as Monterey. On this adventure Irving seems aware of the thinness of his case for the captain and tosses his narrative in with the rest of the journal almost casually, quite as though he had concluded that the less said the better. All in all the captain seems to have had a good time and to have accomplished little else.

A bird of quite another feather who appeared in the Rockies at the same time as Bonneville was Prince Maximilian of Wied-Neuwied. Maximilian was a soldier; he had fought at Jena where he had been captured by the French but was released in time to take part in the triumphal entry into Paris after Napoleon's collapse. He had been well trained and was a scholar and scientist, ethnologist, botanist, geographer, linguist, and he had plenty of money. He cherished no illusions about trapping on the side, as had Bonneville. His was a scientific expedition prepared to pay its own way; it included Charles Bodmer, a Swiss artist paid by Maximilian.

He was especially interested in the Indians and recorded his observations with much care. He saw something of the Mandans and noted the details of their lodges and villages, so different from the tepees of the plains nomads. The Mandans built their houses of clay plastered on a wicker frame and set in compact orderly fashion for mutual aid and defense. He noticed their friendly ways and good manners but ventured no guess as to their ethnological history. Father de Smet thought he detected traces of Winnebago speech among them.

Maximilian concluded that the Aricaras were a branch of the Pawnees and found the men arrogant and unfriendly, but called attention to the attractiveness of the women. He quotes Long's estimate of the total Sioux population as 56,100, all branches, with 14,055 warriors. Like most guesses on Indian numbers this was probably a considerable overestimate. He found pieces of mastodon fossils in an outcropping formation on Milk River, but none in good condition.

Maximilian visited the Crows and was much impressed with them. The men were tall and handsome and carried their heads high and proudly but were generally friendly to the whites. The women, he noted, were good looking and skilful in leather work and the making of bead and feather ornaments. He was fortunate in seeing the Mandans when he did. Three or four years later the great smallpox epidemic of 1837 practically destroyed the tribe. That was a tragic year for the tribes along the Upper Missouri. Among the Assiniboines and the Blackfeet whole villages were wiped out, a fourth of the Pawnees died. The Commissioner of Indian Affairs guessed that among the Upper Missouri people 17,000 Indians died. The Crows suffered least.

Maximilian missed the Nez Perces, the wisest horsemen of them all. The Crows may have practiced selective horse stealing wherever possible and made of it a fine art, but the Nez Perces alone developed selective breeding. The result was the Appaloosa, the best of the Indian ponies. These were famous for their sureness of foot, their speed, and their intelligence. Reliable contemporary descriptions suggest an animal resembling the Palomino the favorite among Mexican horsemen.

A condensed summary of this act that was unfolding of necessity fails to take into account the lone individuals who set the traps and brought in the pelts. Without these Mountain Men, as they were soon called, the fur trade would have lacked color and human reality. What were they like, these lone wanderers? They were young, although some of them lived to grow old before the prosperous days were done. They were wifeless, they were bold, reckless, and hungry for adventure and the chance of wealth. Most of them came up the Missouri in the earlier days, creeping along with sweeps or poles, with days of towing on the cordelle, sometimes but rarely with sails, to the head of navigation of the Missouri. All of them were green, but they learned fast or they died. They dodged Indians or they "forted up" and fought them, often they married Indian women, but seldom for long. These were men who could match the Indians in woodcraft and the gentle art of keeping their hair in a time and place where it was easily lost.

Usually they traveled in pairs or groups of three or four. Killing beaver was a one-man business. Whether singly or in couples they went on foot usually; horses were a constant temptation to Indians except on long swings such as Jedediah Smith's. Their gear was simple, chiefly a gun, skinning knife, tomahawk, a blanket of some sort, lead, salt, powder, flour (corn meal), flint and steel. Traps of course. Their utensils were of the simplest — frying pan, sauce pan, sometimes a coffee pot. Drinkable coffee and edible bread can be made in a frying pan. In Indian country, and they were seldom anywhere else, they kept their fires small and rolled in their blankets far enough from the fire to reduce the danger of night attack.

As with other men engaged in highly specialized work they developed a vocabulary of their own. Such items as tobacco, extra flint and steel, perhaps a compass were "possibles" carried in a buckskin pouch lashed to the belt. Dislike was expressed by a curt phrase, "That don't shine with me!" The setting of a beaver trap gave them the term "That's the way the stick floats," meaning that was the way things looked. The word for a big feed was "doin's," "buffalo doin's," "corn doin's." "Waugh!" was emphatic approval or agreement. Unnecessary adornment, a bright cloth at the neck or around the head, anything beyond the bounds of the strictly utilitarian, was "foofarrow," possibly a mountain colloquialism for "folderol." They soon learned enough Indian sign talk to serve their need; all in all it was a surprisingly self-sufficient life.

Their work was hard and dangerous and they knew that death walked beside them, seldom more than arms length or the length of a rifle barrel away, but they saw the mountains as they had been for geologic ages — clear and shining in the sun, flaming with yellow aspens in autumn or shrouded in winter snows. If they had held high esthetic standards they would never have ventured so far from civilization or the gentler arts of living. They were inarticulate and gave no hint that they saw the beauty around them, but they stayed in spite of the loneliness and their occasional trips down river were unable to break the spell that bound them. They saw the country new and unspoiled, but they had no words for its savage beauty. Waugh!

ILLUSTRATIONS

Plate I. John Colter, discoverer of Yellowstone, running for his life.

Plate II.   "Hard on the heels of the explorers came the trappers and traders." *Page* 20.

Plate III.   "The life of a boatman on the Missouri was not a merry one." *Page* 31.

Plate IV.   "Forty-seven won through to the end of the trail."   *Page 76.*

Plate V. "By 1843 the tide moving toward Oregon began to suggest a traffic jam."
Page 80.

Plate VI. "The drivers were the best that could be found and were inordinately proud of their skill." *Page* 91.

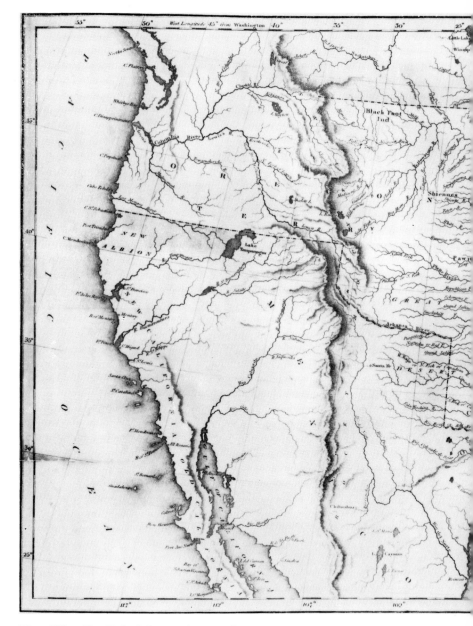

Plate VII.   The United States, circa 1824.

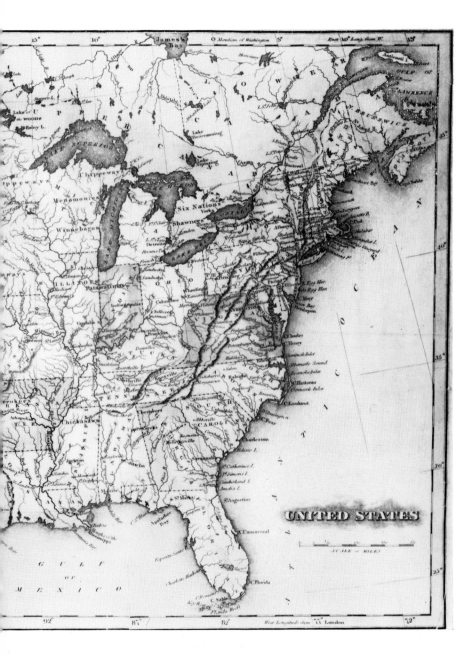

UNITED STATES

Plate VIII. "Fares were high, Atchison to Placerville $225.00." *Page* 91.

Plate IX. "The Pony Express was a gallant experiment." *Page* 95.

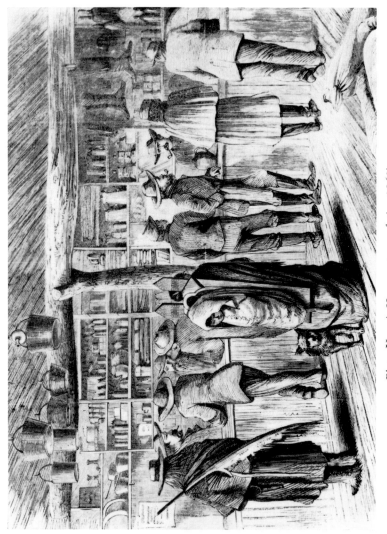

Plate X.   A Kansas store of the 1860's.

Plate XI.   Windmill at Laramie for supplying locomotives of Union Pacific with water.

Plate XII.   Meeting of locomotives of the Union and Central Pacific lines.

Plate XIII. "What was it the engines said?" *Page* 157.

❖❖❖❖❖❖❖❖❖❖❖❖❖❖❖❖❖❖❖❖❖❖❖❖❖❖

CHAPTER V

"Old" Joe Meek

W HEN THE day of the beaver ended the mountain men faced a question for which most of them had no answer. Where do we go from here? A few of them became guides for covered wagons rolling through the mountains to Oregon where wheels were not supposed to go. A number of them, especially those with Indian wives, stayed on in the mountains hunting for meat and occasional pelts, more Indian than white. Bridger made out with his trading post, a center of information for wagon trains, Mormons, argonauts, and wanderers. Jedediah Smith, one of the best, died on the Cimarron. Kit Carson, another good one and more ambitious than most, became a major with General Kearny in the fighting around San Diego in the war with Mexico and a brigadier general for gallant services during the Civil War. Many mountain men simply disappeared, merging with the nameless drifters of that restless time.

One of them, "Old" Joe Meek, made a bargain of his own with the new way of life and wrote his name indelibly into the early history of the Oregon Territory. Meek was born in Virginia in 1810 and while still a youth ran away from home and signed on with William Sublette to go trapping. That an unknown lad of eighteen with no experience should have attracted the attention of a Sublette was a recommendation to any man who knew the mountains or the Sublettes. Most of our knowledge of the melodramatic experiences that followed we owe to a book published in 1870, "The River of the West," written by Mrs. Frances Fuller Victor.

Mrs. Victor talked at length with Joe, at that time a lively youngster of sixty, and found him a mine of reminiscence with no taint of modesty or undue reticence. It is Mrs. Victor who tells us of Joe's remark to an English traveler who asked him how long he had been in Oregon: "When I first come to this country Mount Hood was a hole in the ground." That is still a classic of Northwest legendry, with many claimants for the honor of having said it first. Another yarn that Meek confided to Mrs. Victor was of preaching to the Nez Perces for a fee of thirteen horses, many beaver skins, and a Nez Perce girl as a wife. This one had a core of truthfulness; at least he had a Nez Perce wife, although two children had been born to the happy pair before Joe found time for a wedding ceremony. Another time he claimed to have prayed half an hour for a cow. At least he had a cow.

He was a good bit of a clown and his love of truth was easily kept under control. Once a mad wolf came into camp and bit two or three men before he was put out of action. Meek was drunk and when one of his companions told him that in his helpless condition he might well have been a victim Meek brushed the danger aside: "It would have cured the wolf sure — if it hadn't killed him."

Clown as he may have been and often drunk by his own admission, but he was a stiff fighter, too. He was in the thick of a bloody fight with the Blackfeet in Pierre's Hole and after an ambush on Pryor's River he showed eleven bullet holes in the blanket that he carried draped over his arm. Even in the midst of his fighting he kept his sense of humor. In an ambush on the Yellowstone his mule balked and he shouted to his companions: "Hold on, boys. There ain't many of them. Let's stop and fight 'em." At that moment the smell of Indians stirred his stubborn steed to action and as he rushed past his fleeing mates Meek yelled back: "Run for your lives, boys. There's ten thousand of them. They'll kill every one of you!"

You may be sure that Old Joe saw to it in his stories that he got none the worst of it. Once he told of being attacked by an indignant grizzly at such close range that he thrust the muzzle of his gun into the animal's mouth. Ephraim slapped the gun away with a swing of his paw. Joe drew his knife and that too the bear sent spinning. Finally he finished his antagonist off with his ready tomahawk. Probably if the axe had been lost he would have done the job with his teeth.

Like other mountain men Joe had lots of excitement but no money and also like the others he lost his heart to the beautiful Mrs. Whitman. Later as the first United States marshal in Oregon Territory he had the satisfaction of hanging the Cayuses convicted of the killings at Waiilatpu. The acting governor, an old friend, had intimated his intention of commuting the death sentence to life imprisonment. Joe said drily: "As far as Meek is concerned he would do anything for you . . . I have got in my pocket the death warrant of them Indians, signed by Governor Lane. The marshal will hang them men as certain as the day arrives." And hanged they were.

The marshal might be informal in his manner but he had no fear of his job. The captain of a British ship had once ordered him ashore in the harbor of Portland. After he had become marshal, Joe had evidence that the captain was doing a spot of smuggling. Now it was different. The captain greeted him with marked courtesy and inquired politely: "Haven't I met you before?" The answer was quick and curt: "I was nothing but Joe Meek then and you ordered me ashore. I am now Colonel Joseph L. Meek, United States Marshal for this Territory of Oregon, and you, sir, are only a damned smuggler. Go ashore, sir!"

Meek knew when to temper justice with discretion. Dr. White, the Indian agent, tried to levy on a barrel of whiskey in the possession of an English woman, a Madam Cooper. The offender chased the agent down the trail with a hot poker and when Meek, the sheriff, appeared the poker was still in evidence and still hot. Joe made peace talk. "As I am not quite so high an authority as Dr. White about a quart will do me."

There is no doubt of the Meek prowess as a trapper and Indian fighter, even after due allowance is made for his soaring imagination, but it is hard to believe that he found much time to work his trap line between fights with Blackfeet and Crows. Nevertheless his standing in the trapping world was high as more than one expert could testify. Such judges as Jim Bridger and Broken Hand Kilpatrick were not easy to fool.

It was as guide and official in Oregon that he won his greatest and most lasting fame. He even took time to acquire a farm in the Willamette valley. In March of 1843, a meeting of settlers at Champoeg voted to organize a government on the spot and Meek was elected sheriff. His widespread reputation, his easy manner, and his abundant nerve made him an irresistible candidate.

The meeting at Champoeg was only a first step toward territorial status, although Oregon was still under joint British-American control. Polk was president and someone must go to Washington to lay Oregon's claim before the president. Of course there was only one man who could do the job; that was "Old" Joe Meek. He knew the mountains and the Indians and he had the added qualification of being a cousin of James K.

Polk. At the start of the trip Joe had six companions, but two of them lost their nerve and decided that Fort Boise looked like a good place to spend the winter. The others stuck. There must have been many narrow squeaks in the dangerous stretches, but the record remains of only one or two. Once he and his mates blundered into a Sioux village in a driving snowstorm and got through by the simple process of going on, the storm being severe enough to keep even the Indian dogs under cover. Provisions ran low and Meek afterwards told with great glee of the time when their menu consisted of two polecats roasted over the coals of a small fire.

The time from Portland to St. Joseph, Missouri, was two months and the travelers were penniless, ragged, and hungry but Joe remembered that the father of one of his Oregon friends lived in St. Joe and straightway sought him out. The result was funds enough to carry them to St. Louis. From St. Louis to Washington by steamboat and stage fares loomed as an impassable barrier, but not for Joe. Competing steamboats lay at the St. Louis wharves taking on cargo and passengers for the run down the Mississippi and up the Ohio to Pittsburgh and Joe, arrayed in mountain clothes, took his stand by the gangplank of his choice and delivered himself of this oration:

"This way, gentlemen, if you please. Come right on board the *Declaration*. I am the man from Oregon, with dispatches to the President of these United States, that you all read about in this morning's paper. Come on board, ladies and gentlemen, if you want to hear the news from Oregon. I've just come across the plains, two months from the Columbia River, where the Injuns are killing your missionaries. Those passengers who come aboard the *Declaration* shall hear all about it before they get to Pittsburgh. Don't stand thar lookin' at my old wolfskin cap, but just come aboard and hear what I've got to tell."

The boat was delayed by high water in the Ohio and when they reached Pittsburgh they found that the regular stage to Washington had already left. Meek talked himself and the others in a special coach to Washington, thereby adding to his already large popularity with his fellow passengers. Polk hailed him as a long lost cousin and put pressure on Congress to pass the bill establishing the Oregon Territory as soon as the treaty with Great Britain was signed. As soon as that was done Old Joe was promptly named as the first United States marshal of the new Territory. The old Mountain Man had become one of the builders of a new commonwealth. Few trappers of beaver could match this.

CHAPTER VI

The Road to Oregon

THE MOUNTAIN men had two fixed beliefs to which they all subscribed. One was that wagon wheels would never cross the Rockies, perhaps a natural result of their pride in their own skill and hardihood as trailmakers. They knew the mountains at first hand and that was all that was necessary for their conclusion. Daniel Webster, who knew nothing of mountains except the tame ones of his native state, agreed with them on the inaccessibility of the country beyond the Rockies and the folly of a wrangle with the British over title to it.

The other article in the creed of the mountain men was that the supply of beaver was inexhaustible and that there would be a market for the fur as long as men of fashion needed it for high crowned hats, and that would be forever. Before they died many of the mountain men guided wagon trains through the mountains where they had said wagon wheels would never roll.

The belief in the immortality of the beaver trade was equally flimsy. Only Astor read the writing on the wall. On his frequent visits to London he heard increasingly of the silk hats that were being turned out in Paris and in 1834 he announced his own retirement and transferred the active control of his interests to some of his former associates and partners, Sublette, Bridger, and others. The trade continued but the pace of it visibly slackened and after the last great rendezvous of 1840 it declined steadily in importance.

Three years before Astor withdrew from the mountain trade steam had appeared on the Upper Missouri. This was the steamboat *Yellowstone* that left St. Louis in 1831, forerunner of the flatbottomed stern-wheelers that were to add their bit to the history of the Big Muddy. It was the boast of their captains that these shallow draft pioneers could run on a heavy fall of dew.

There was good reason for the overlapping of the day of the beaver with the era of the Oregon emigrant and the covered wagon. Trappers knew their way through and among the mountains, but they were not trailmakers or markers. They sought only beaver and were more concerned with keeping their knowledge to themselves than blazoning it abroad. A remote stream filled with beaver was their idea of an earthly paradise and if it was also moderately free of danger from Indians so much the better. More than a few times they set traps along streams where later comers found gold in abundance, but the trappers ignored such possibilities as they did the presence of fertile soil that the emigrants coveted. The mountain men who found work guiding wagons through old beaver country to the Columbia were merely amused by such reckless folly. Bridger took Brigham Young and his "Pioneers" to the Salt Lake valley and offered the Mormon leader a dollar an ear for all the corn he would ever grow in that arid land. Fortunately for Bridger betting is against Mormon principles.

It is strange that the earliest definite impulse to find a way for wheels through the mountains should have been given by a missionary on his way to found a mission among the Indians on the Columbia. The man was Marcus Whitman, trained to be a doctor and determined to carry the gospel along with his medicines to the savages of the Northwest. The story of Whitman makes most historical novels seem dull and spiritless. Four strange Indians, later identified as Flatheads and Nez Perces, appeared in St. Louis and made their way to the hospitable home of William Clark of the Lewis and Clark partnership. To Clark all Indians were friends and when he found that the fathers of these wanderers had taked with the explorers and that the sons had come to ask for teachers who could talk to them about God he gave them special welcome.

Strange Indians were nothing new in St. Louis, but these four attracted much attention because of their errand. A considerable body of legend sprang up about their visit, most of which is apocryphal. One story is of a speech made by one of them at a farewell banquet given them by William Clark. Solely because of its picturesqueness and pathos it is worth repeating:

"I come to you over the trail of many moons from the setting sun. You were the friends of my fathers, who have all gone the long way. I came with an eye partly open for my people who sit in darkness. I go back with both eyes closed. How can I go back blind to my blind people? I made my way to you with strong arms through many enemies and strange lands that I might carry back much to them. I go back with both arms broken and empty. Two fathers came with us. We leave them asleep here by your great waters and wigwams. They were tired in many moons and their moccasins wore out.

"My people sent me to get the 'White Man's Book of Heaven.' You took me to where you allow your women to dance, as we do not ours, and the book was not there. You took me to where you worship the Great Spirit with candles and the book was not there. You showed me images of the good spirits and the picture of the good land beyond, but the book is not among them to tell us the way. I am going back the long sad trail to my people in the dark land. You make my feet heavy with gifts and my moccasins will grow old carrying them, yet the book is not among them. When I tell my poor blind people, after one more snow, in the big council, that I did not bring the book, no word will be spoken by our old men or by our young braves. One by one they will rise and go out in silence. My people will die in darkness, and they will go a long path to other hunting grounds. No white man will go with them, and no white man's book to make the way plain. I have no more words."

It would be pleasant to record that such words were spoken on such an occasion, but it wouldn't be true. The sober facts are that four Indians came to William Clark, headquarters for all friendless Indians, two of them died there, and doubtless there was a feast and much smoking of the pipe of friendship. That was Indian ritual. What we know to have happened was that the mission people began to sit up and take notice.

Word of the errand of these Indians from across the mountains soon reached Whitman and he at once determined to answer the call, although he knew nothing of the mountain country or of the Northwest generally. In his application to the mission board he had confessed present bachelorhood but stated that he had an open mind on the subject of matrimony. "I am not marrid and I have no present arangement upon that Subject. Yet I should wish to take a wife, if the service of the Board would admit." Such "arangements" take time and the Board was pressing; time was of the essence. So Whitman set forth in company with the Rev. Samuel Parker to spy out this distant land of Canaan; Lucien Fontenelle, the best of Astor's caravan leaders, was head of this preliminary reconnaissance.

On the way the advance agents stopped off briefly to view the fur rendezvous in the valley of the Green. Parker in his journal describes in some detail the famous duel between Kit Carson and the bully of the mountains, Shunar. This is another of the mountain episodes that has passed into the realm of the legendary. It is certain that there was such a duel, not an unusual occurrence at a rendezvous, but it was probably not the romantic affair that some of the versions made it. One such relation states that Carson fought to protect the honor of a beautiful Arapaho maiden who became his wife. It is sure that Kit's first wife was Indian and that they lived together until her death. More than that is mostly fiction.

Kit Carson was one of the mountain men who needed no aura of legend to gild his fame. There were Carsons with the Kentucky hunters who came to Missouri early and pushed farther on as opportunity offered. Kit was apprenticed to a saddle maker in St. Joe and yielded easily to the tempting of the mountain country, breaking his articles of apprenticeship at the age of fifteen to ride herd on the spare remuda of a wagon train bound for Santa Fe. His employer offered fifty cents for his return and within a year was himself bound for Santa Fe. Kit's nickname among mountain men was Bub, an allusion to the slender, youthful look that he never lost. The war with Mexico sent him to California as a mixture of guide and hunter with Kearny and brought him the brevet rank of major for his part in the bloody scramble around San Diego.

By anyone's standard Kit Carson was one of the best. If one brackets with his the names of Jim Bridger and "Broken Hand" Fitzpatrick he will probably have named the three greatest of the Mountain Men, men who could do anything anyone else could do and do it better.

Returning to Whitman, Parker reports that the young doctor performed a surgical operation on Bridger, cutting a Blackfoot arrowhead out of his shoulder. Parker says of this: "The doctor pursued the operation with great self-possession and persistence; and his patient manifested equal firmness." Whitman made no mention of either of these occurrences.

Back at his home in New York, Whitman set about the preparations for the trip to his chosen mission in the Oregon country, including courtship and marriage. The young lady of his choice was Narcissa Prentiss who had already applied for a missionary assignment and had been accepted as Parker's assistant. The marriage took place in February, 1836, and the happy pair left at once on their long honeymoon, ninety-six days from the Missouri to the Columbia. The Whitmans took with them the Rev. Henry Harmon Spalding and his wife, a layman William H. Gray, from Utica, and two Indians whom Whitman had brought with him on his return from the survey trip. They also took with them Whitman's determination to prove that wagons could cross the mountains. There were four milk cows in the Whitman entourage and fresh milk for children and invalids. Narcissa baked fresh bread every evening, another new thing for the trail.

The caravan assembled at the junction of the Loup River and the Platte. It was surely a strange company that set forth to accomplish the feat that Webster and the mountain men had declared impossible. To begin with it was enough to expect two women to endure the hardships of the long journey without further complicating the ordeal with wagons. There were the usual trappers and traders to whom were added the missionaries and a wealthy English sportsman Sir William Drummond Stewart with servants and dogs bound on a big game hunt. Sir William was a familiar figure in mountain country. Narcissa found this an experience of unalloyed pleasure. She was an accomplished horsewoman and the days passed all too quickly. Mrs. Spalding was a semi-invalid with neurotic tendencies who must have taken an exceedingly dim view of the whole affair. To many of the white men in the caravan they were the first white women they had seen in months and to the Indians they met along the way the first in their lives. At the head of the company was Thomas Fitzpatrick who spoke Indian with an Irish accent and thought little of the wagons.

Somewhere along the trail, perhaps at the River Loup, the Whitman cavalcade acquired another odd recruit, a sixteen-year-old boy, Miles Goodyear, traveling alone, his only outfit, the clothes he wore. As to destination he knew only that it was somewhere west and he seemed to have no doubt of his ability to get there. He too lacked sympathy with the wagon project and finally broke with Whitman over this and became a capable mountain man. Boys became men fast in that country or they didn't last. Goodyear's final phase was as a farmer in the Salt Lake desert, the first to raise a crop in that forlorn land. His farm was on the site of the present city of Ogden.

For a long time the pro-Whitmanites had a gaudy wrangle with the antis over the Whitman accomplishments or the lack of them. Did he or did he not make good on his vow to take wagon wheels through the mountains? At its best such an argument has little merit and in view of his solid work at Waiilatpu and the tragic sequel of November 29, 1847, even less than that. For whatever it may be worth this is how the record stands: Yielding to Fitzpatrick's urging one of the two wagons that started from the River Loup was abandoned at Fort Laramie. The other took a bad beating and came to Fort Boise only half a wagon. The front wheels had been sacrificed and the vehicle that came through to Boise was a two-wheeled cart, consisting of the axle and rear wheels of the original, and even this went no further. Whitman's stubbornness had paid the small dividend of wheels over the Continental Divide. It wasn't much but it was something. It is recorded that Capt. Bonneville had taken wagons to the Bear River Rendezvous three years earlier. The point to be remembered about Whitman is that when he established his mission on the Walla Walla he served notice on the British that here was something more than a trading post for a fur company; this was civilization and American at that.

A famous contemporary of Whitman was the wandering missionary priest, Father Pierre Jean de Smet, probably the most widely known and highly regarded white man in all the mountain country. It is an uncertain possibility that these two devoted characters ever met although de Smet went many places and knew many men. It is said that he once presented a copy of the Bible to Whitman, duly inscribed that still exists somewhere. De Smet was born in Belgium and served his novitiate in Baltimore. Soon after its completion he appeared in St. Louis, one of twelve young priests who had traveled from the Chesapeake to the Mississippi by steamboat and on foot. That was in 1823 when the fur trade in the Upper Missouri country was booming. The Jesuit order had established a new Province in the region beyond the Mississippi and de Smet organized a Novitiate at Florissant about fifteen miles from St. Louis, destined to be the germ of the powerful St. Louis University.

From that time until his death in 1873 he divided his time between travels among the Indians, counseling them, holding services, conciliating hostile tribes, establishing small missions, and making trips to Europe for financial support and recruits for his missions. He knew Indians and he dealt bluntly with foolish friends who sought to load him down with inappropriate gifts for his savage parishioners. He was threatened with a bishopric but dodged it. Not for him the miter and the solemn ceremony. He talked with many chiefs and warriors as well as white men of all kinds and stations, but his first concern was always Indians. He never forgot that he was a priest and not an explorer or an advance agent of civilization. He dealt with the Indians as he found them, candidates for salvation, although he had his doubts about the implacable Blackfeet. In a letter to his Provincial Father he says of them: "The Blackfeet are the only Indians of whose salvation we would have reason to despair if the ways of God were the same as those of man, for they are murderers, thieves, traitors, and all that is wicked."

Father de Smet was tireless in his travels among the Indians in spite of frequent appeals from the head of the province to help in raising funds and recruits for the novitiate at Florissant. It has been said that in the course of his life he covered a distance equal to twice the circumference of the earth. That seems a bit on the extreme side, but it is certain that he covered ground. Most of his travels in Indian country were on foot, occasionally on a horse or by canoe. He was a big man, two hundred and fifteen pounds. Warned that he was overweight for snowshoe travel he got rid of thirty pounds in a month by fasting and exercise.

Of this aspect of his work he wrote: "I have been for years a wanderer in the desert. I was three years without receiving a letter from any quarter. I was two years in the mountains without tasting bread, salt, coffee, tea, sugar. I was for years without a roof, without a bed. I have been six months without a shirt on my back and often have I passed whole days and nights without a morsel of anything to eat."

When necessary he traveled alone or with an Indian guide through savage country where death in a variety of ways walked beside him. Sometimes he acted as an unofficial and unpaid emissary of the Government. He urged upon the Indians the necessity of peace with each other and with the whites. In all his contacts with the Government he stressed the importance of prompt payment of annuities promised to the Indians and the providing of tools and seed. Always he urged justice and honesty in all dealings with Indians. He denounced the trade in alcohol and sought to convince the savages of the need of Christian marriage instead of the traditional practice of purchase. And of course he preached salvation everywhere.

He went in and out among discordant tribes with no sign of fear and never was there a hint of a threat by any Indian against Black Robe, as they called him. Testimony is universal that here at least was one white man that all the Indians trusted, even the fierce Blackfeet. After one council a chief said to him: "If it had been any other white man than you, Black Robe, this day would have been his last." Indian practice called for much eating as a token of friendliness. Visiting the Crows on the Bighorn he was the guest of honor and recorded "twenty banquets in one afternoon," an ordeal for a man who must watch his weight. At the age of sixty-eight he traveled with only an Indian guide three hundred and fifty miles through country bristling with hostiles thirsty for white blood to talk with Sitting Bull, the firebrand of the Sioux. Fortunately he did not live to see the ruin of his fondest hopes on the Little Bighorn three years after he died.

In all his work and words de Smet was singularly selfless and devoted. In the history of the Northwest he is without a peer.

The way the Oregon emigrants traveled — and the way that the Whitmans went — was over the high plateau that Stuart found with his message to Astor, now called South Pass. Except for stiffish climbs at the eastern and western ends it bore little resemblance to the typical mountain pass which suggests narrow trails, high mountains, and deep canyons. South Pass was twenty miles wide most of the way over and the point where the western slope began, the Continental Divide, was hardly perceptible to the traveler. The chief problem was water — or the lack of it. Where any was to be found it was generally heavily alkaline and seldom drinkable. In Whitman's time there was little danger from Indians; that was to come later when Sioux and Arapaho concluded that they must fight to hold this land of their fathers.

The emigrants bound for Oregon or California who followed at Whitman's heels found this level, treeless gateway through the mountains something beyond their understanding. But as traffic grew landmarks began to be located and named; Courthouse Rock that some homesick migrant thought looked like the familiar county courthouse now so far back, Independence Rock, a massive whale-back of stone outcropping on this barren prairie. Why Independence? One explanation is that a covered wagon outfit camped near the rock on July the Fourth and celebrated the day by christening the rock. Most trains stopped long enough to give the men of the party a chance to scratch initials, a date, the name of a home town to show that humanity was passing that way. It was so that Spanish missionary friars marked their pilgrimages through the deserts of the Southwest — *"Paso por aqui"* (there passed by here) — with a name and a date. It wasn't much perhaps, but these faint scratches became part of the record of time and place.

There were other landmarks and known spots, sometimes with grass, wood, and water. Chimney Rock was a feature that nearly all keepers of journals mentioned. This could be seen from a distance of forty miles and its height was estimated at around three hundred feet. Palmer, the leader of one of the wagon trains, recorded that it had the "unpoetical appear-

ance of a haystack with a pole running far above its top."
Scott's Bluffs appeared in most of the diaries, as did the Devil's
Gate. This was one of the landmarks that really looked the part
of a mountain pass. Chittenden says of it: "This remarkable
feature is a rift in a granite ridge through which the river flows.
It is about four hundred feet deep, with sides nearly vertical,
and less than three hundred feet wide at the top. It is the most
notable feature of its kind in the world."

The most important point on the way for these far wanderers was neither a high rock nor a narrow canyon but a post,
Fort Laramie. Here was a stockade and safety, a place to rest,
to replenish slender stocks of supplies, sometimes fresh oxen,
seldom if ever horses or mules. The first post here was built by
Robert Campbell and was christened Fort William in honor
of Campbell's partner William L. Sublette. Two years later it
became an American Fur Company post and was renamed
Fort John after John B. Sarpy. It became an army post in 1849
and was given the name of Fort Laramie, after a shadowy figure Jacques Laramie about whom nothing is known except
that he is supposed to have come into Wyoming about 1820 and
to have been killed by Indians soon after. Perhaps the mystery
surrounding this man was the reason for the army's choice of a
name. At least no one could charge them with playing army
favorites. It remained an army post until 1890 when the Indian danger was long past.

❖❖❖❖❖❖❖❖❖❖❖❖❖❖❖❖❖❖❖❖❖❖❖❖❖❖❖❖

CHAPTER VII

Covered Wagon People

CLOSE behind Whitman came the covered wagons, important features of the American saga. Novelists and filmmakers have given to the life of these emigrants a color and flavor of romance that was not apparent at the time. Doubtless there were a few fiddles and banjos in the wagons but their evenings were not spent in dancing about the campfires to the music of "Old Dan Tucker" and the "Arkansas Traveler." There were repairs to be made on harness and wagons, food to prepare, plans to be made for the next day's ordeal. These were sober people and many of the songs they sang were hymns. There were prayer meetings and occasionally a funeral. Cholera traveled with them in the early forties, as far as Laramie, and life was a grim and serious business.

They came mostly from north of the Ohio and a surprising number began the long trek in upstate New York or even New England. They knew what they wanted — land, homes, and a wider sky. They were not of the stuff of which adventurers are made but family people with children and a vision of communities with churches and schools, perhaps even colleges, in that far land. The Yankees among them gave a distinctly New England flavor which is still to be found in the older parts of Oregon. Few of the covered wagon folk had anything that could be called capital — bits of furniture, bedding, simple cooking utensiles, necessary clothing, guns of course, a milk cow or two; more than once a meek old bossie was pressed into service as a draft animal.

Whether bound for California or Oregon the people in the covered wagons traveled in the midst of danger, storm, hunger, thirst, sickness, accident, Indians. Those who followed the advice of the mountain men, the old-timers who knew the country, generally fared the best, although even these wise ones had few guarantees of safe conduct. In general the better the outfit the easier the life of the trail, but even this rule did not always hold good. Take the case of the Donner party from Sangamon County in Illinois. Here was something rare along the trail, whether to Oregon or to California. George Donner the patriarch was sixty-two years old and a man of considerable means. Born in North Carolina he had known Kentucky, Illinois, Indiana, Texas, and now Illinois again and wherever he stopped he acquired land, wives, and children, thirteen children from three wives. Tamsen, wife number three, had three children aged six, four, and three. She was a person of talent, education, and pluck as she was to demonstrate abundantly on the way to California. Incidentally she took with her $10,000 in bank notes stitched into the lining of a quilt. There were three Donner brothers, each with three wagons. James Frazier Reed, another Sangamon County settler who was joining the party, also had three. Reed's family vehicle had bunks and a stove; also a supply of wine and brandy. Not all the members of the party as it finally assembled for the start were of this caliber. At least four of them were teamsters for George Donner. Others had more modest outfits, although Patrick Breen from Keokuk, Iowa, with his six sons had his three wagons and an oversupply of what passed for luxuries among emigrants.

Why did such successful people pull up their stakes in a land where they had already succeeded beyond the lot of the average settelr? Part of the reason was undoubtedly the stories they had heard of the California climate, a land flowing with milk and honey, bathed in golden sunshine, a coveted boon to people who had known the cold winters and bleak springs of the Illinois country. At this time, 1846, much weight must be given to the magic of the words California and Oregon. When so many people were on the move it was not easy to close one's ears. After all life on an Illinois farm can be drab and dull, and too many of the western tales that filled the air were concocted of the stuff that dreams are made of; too few of them told of the endless miles and days, sagebrush, alkaline water, rattlesnakes, hunger.

It was the bad luck of the Donner party to come under the influence of the most dangerous dreamer of them all. That was one Lansford Hastings. Born in Mount Vernon, Ohio, he had elected himself as the chief boomer for California. Hastings remains an elusive figure in the California story, part real estate operator, part politician seeking power, part restless adventurer, and a considerable part plain liar. Among other misty illusions was the "Hastings cutoff" from Fort Bridger to the southern end of Great Salt Lake and then due west to what he called the Ogden's River country, probably the Humboldt. Although he knew little of his proposed route, chiefly the part nearest to Fort Bridger, he wrote glibly of the ease of travel by it and assured his readers that they need have no fear of the Sierras; reports of heavy snows in the mountains and steep climbs over the top were mostly Oregon publicity. His cutoff was not only easy traveling but it was at least three hundred and fifty miles shorter than any other.

Hastings was always about to meet the Donners on the way to his promised land but he was always too busy somewhere else. Hastings or no Hastings the Donners left Fort Bridger on July 31, eighty-seven in number, thirty-six of them under eighteen years old. They reached the Great Salt Lake August 27 after a heartbreaking struggle through the Wasatch, an almost impossible route for wagons. From there on the record of each day's travel was the same, impossible trails, breakdowns, quarrels with each other. The inevitable feuds began to appear. October was behind them when they reached Truckee Lake. In the meantime they had been forced to abandon wagons because of lack of draft animals, food was almost gone, the hardest climb of all was ahead of them, and winter was coming fast. Three months from Fort Bridger to Truckee Meadows, nearly the time for a normal crossing from Independence to Sacramento.

The ghastly story of the Donners has been told more than often enough. It is filled with courage, cowardice, meanness, self-sacrifice, weakness, and endurance beyond belief. Worst of all there was cannibalism, not for the first time in the long history of westward wandering. Finally the end of the suffering was reached when the survivors were brought down the western slope of the Sierras. It was the end of April. There had been eighty-two of them at Truckee. Forty-seven won through to the end of the trail.

Was the misleading, elusive Hastings the sole cause for the appalling experience of this elaborately equipped, well-financed party? Hardly! In sober truth the elaborate equipment was an important contribution to their vulnerability. Some of the wagons were unnecessarily large. One was called the Ark. It had bunks, chairs, a stove, quantities of bedding, books that Tamsen was taking to California for the school that she planned to establish in the new land. Reed took with him a store of wine, brandy, and other delicacies for the trail. Luxuries had no proper place on the road they were to travel.

Of course Hastings deceived them, but they were unusually credulous and they wanted to believe. James Clymer, one of the best mountain men and a teller of the truth, warned them away from the Hastings cutoff as did that other old-timer Bridger, but their elaborate outfit and their dream of California sunshine had conditioned them for the Hastings blandishments. Frankly theirs was the old story of the siren and the sucker.

There was considerable argument over the proper draft animals for the long pull, especially over the relative merits of the ox and the mule. Southerners generally voted for the mule while New Englanders plumped for oxen as more familiar and reliable. There were few backers of the horse although there were many horses traveling the trail generally under the saddle. A favorite argument of the mule party was that there was less liability of Indians stealing a mule for food, an assumption that ignored the willingness of the redskin to eat mule meat, ox, or horse, whichever was available. On the trail oxen outpointed mules at least two to one. Two miles an hour was a good pace for oxen, but they could be counted on to deliver the miles through a long day, given halfway decent going. They were steady on the hard pulls while the mule was temperamental, and easily discouraged. The mule also dreaded mud, although mud was not common through the mountains or in the desert. A few teapot tempests blew up over dogs. On at least one occasion a proposal was made to shoot all the dogs because they would attract the attention of the Indians by their barking. A few dogs were killed but the owners served notice that any further killing would be paid in kind by the pro-dog men.

The covered wagons offered no space for large heirlooms or for purely sentimental or decorative articles; the first shipload on the *Mayflower* had fewer perhaps, but not by much. Even so the emigrant tracks were strewn with broken or discarded pieces no longer necessary enough to deserve a place in the creaking, rickety wagons. Some of the more prosperous were able to procure the services of men who had been trappers and knew the country and its savage peoples. Many were forced to find their way from such traces of predecessors as they could not help seeing. The wonder was that so many won through; they were the ones who planted civilization to stay in the Northwest.

Wherever their homes had been the wagon people gathered mostly at St. Joseph, Missouri, where they joined other families and groups for the long jump westward. Their organization was of the simplest sort, a captain chosen by vote to make the few decisions of places to lay over for the night or for a longer period of rest and repair, occasional choices of routes, although in general the way was fairly evident. Wagons wore out, wheels dried in the hot sun of the High Plains; where trees were found new parts could be contrived, tires reset, tongues or felloes hewn from green wood. Sometimes wagons were beyond repair and people and goods doubled up as best they could.

Some captains of trains were good, some poor, most of them a fair average that learned as it drove. It is a striking feature of the American story that the spirit that generated the Mayflower Compact should appear so often in our history in such strange guises and at such times of need. It is a story of free men on the move taking the law with them or making it to suit the needs of the day.

Few of them had been able to visualize the tremendous distance in terms of days and weeks, two thousand miles with fifteen miles a good day's performance, more often ten or less. For most of them the route followed was up the Platte from that river's junction with the Missouri, over to the North Fork of the Platte where Fort Kearney soon appeared, and so to the

high, dry plateau of South Pass.   Important as was Fort Laramie to the covered wagon people, Fort Hall, in present Idaho,
was even more critical.   Here or near here a decision must be
made. California or Oregon? Gold had not yet been found
as the magic lure drawing men to California, but more than
a few voted for the Land of Sunshine, for no apparent reason
except that it was there.   Most of the wagons continued on
to Oregon even before the treaty with Great Britain had established this as American territory.   Fort Hall had been named
by Wyeth in honor of the oldest man in his company.

The year 1840 saw the appearance of one of the more
fantastic figures in our history, John C. Fremont, an officer
of French descent in the American army.   He had the good
judgment to fall in love with Jessie Benton, the strong-minded
daughter of "Old Bullion" Benton, a senator from Missouri.
Jessie reciprocated and broke the news to her father.   After a
few paternal explosions the Senator wisely submitted to the
inevitable and cast about for a way to use his new son-in-law
to his own good purposes.   He was not long in finding it.
Benton was intoxicated with his own doctrine of Manifest Destiny and the gallant young officer might serve as window dress-
ing. Why not a career as an explorer? It was a career that
Fremont sought and he was not particular about the field.
There must be a lot of country in the Rocky Mountains that
hadn't been examined yet: hence Fremont the Pathfinder who
was led by the hand by Kit Carson through regions that by
that time scores or even hundreds of men knew as they had
known their own barnyards in Missouri.

Fremont found nothing that hadn't already been discovered, but his detailed maps had value. He gave his name to an
unimportant mountain fifty miles off the trail and added
something to the current of humanity that was setting toward
Oregon. His restless feet and hunger for fame soon took him

into California where he played a much disputed part in the pulling and hauling around Sacramento and Monterey that went by the name of the Bear Republic. At least there was a flag bearing the hulking figure of a California grizzly. That wasn't enough for him. When the young Republican party put a candidate for the presidency in the field in 1856 who could it be but Fremont the Pathfinder? When the Civil War precipitated local conflict in Missouri, Fremont was right there as military governor, a post in which he won little distinction. The combination of Benton drive and Fremont thirst for fame was not a happy one but it was exciting.

By 1843, the tide flowing toward Oregon began to suggest traffic jams in the midst of the mountains. Some of the trains were prodigious, the one headed by Peter H. Burnett for example. Burnett, who was to be the first governor of California a decade later, was a young lawyer in Missouri who caught the Oregon fever and in 1843 put together the biggest train of them all, according to his own account more than a hundred wagons, 5,000 cattle, 260 men, 130 women, and 610 children. It was elaborately organized, at least on paper, with captains, sergeants, and a code of laws, but less well in reality. After the manner of Oregon emigrants generally, they quarreled over routes, stopping places, even over ultimate goals. Their immense herd of stock was a perpetual drag and cause of discord and they finally split into two columns, one the Light Column without cattle under William Martin, the other called the Cow Column with Jesse Applegate as captain. Applegate seems to have been something of a dictator with mind fixed solely on getting through to Oregon, and that he did. Later he gave his name to a cutoff from the Humboldt to the Columbia.

This was not the only wagon train of the year, merely the largest, and when Fremont came over on his second trip in

August he found South Pass marked by many roads and of course strewn with the discards and the wreckage of the trail. This time the Pathfinder went as far as the Dalles of the Columbia where he learned that the settlers had organized the Territory of Oregon and heard men speak of Old Joe Meek as the moving spirit in the Americanization of the country. John McLaughlin, head factor for the Hudson's Bay Company, was still Father Christmas for more than one stranded company, but not for long.

By 1846 the movement toward Oregon and northern California, mostly over South Pass, had begun to resemble a mass migration of mixed races, creeds, colors, and purposes — British sportsmen looking for big game, bear, elk, buffalo, traveled in the same brigade with mountain men from Kentucky; lanky, drawling, slouching Missouri farmers weary of a diet of corn pone and malaria, with French Canadian packers and rivermen, and here and there a negro from the docks of St. Louis. The trail to the west drew a cross section of America, even a Boston Brahmin or two. In April of that year Francis Parkman, blue blood from Beacon Hill, and his cousin Quincy Adams Shaw appeared in St. Louis looking for an emigrant outfit to which they could attach themselves. Parkman was especially interested in Indians and was collecting material for his "Conspiracy of Pontiac." Surely there were specimens of the noble red man to be found somewhere along the Oregon Trail. Some of the young Sioux warriors he encountered pleased him more than the white men he traveled with. By the time he reached Fort Laramie he had had enough and his Oregon Trail stopped there, although he was only halfway to the mouth of the Columbia. He added little or nothing to our knowledge of the land or the people, but his *Oregon Trail* is a graphic account of his experiences and impressions.

There have been many arguments over the exact route of the Oregon Trail and many attempts to relocate it. Pre-eminence in these efforts surely belongs to Ezra Meeker of Oregon, a veteran of the trail if there was one. Having traveled it first with his father in 1852 at the age of twenty-one with an ox team, in his old age he devoted himself to repeating that early exodus. In all he covered the route five times after he had reached the ripe age of seventy-six, once in 1906, again with an ox team in 1910, by automobile in 1915, and in an airplane in 1924. Finally in 1928, approaching his ninety-eighth birthday, he tried it again starting from the East in a Ford car. This was his last. Taken ill on the way, his life ended in a hospital in Seattle.

✤✤✤✤✤✤✤✤✤✤✤✤✤✤✤✤✤✤✤✤✤✤✤✤✤✤✤✤

CHAPTER VIII

Mormons, Argonauts and Overland Stages

I T WAS long the practice of American historians to regard
the rise of the Mormon church as an insolent, if not blas-
phemous, interruption of the smooth course of the American
story. This is an attitude hardly to be justified on any reason-
able ground. To be sure Mormonism was a mixture of the
ecclesiastic and the political, but so were other religious movements, Puritanism for example. It had aroused violent criticism and opposition and so had other new beliefs; Quakerism
was one, although Quakers held no principle more revolu-
tionary than the right of every man to walk by his own inner
light.

The early half of the nineteenth century was a period of
new and strange creeds and movements. Belief in the second
coming of Christ was widely prevalent and the Millerites
waited on hilltops in the windy chill of October nights to welcome the promised manifestation, receiving nothing but colds
in the head. Spiritualistic seances were largely attended and
bands of Shakers sought to rid themselves of their sins by means
of the Holy Dance. Followers of Robert Owen taught that
true harmony could be achieved only through cooperation and
founded a colony at New Harmony, Indiana, that exhibited

only internal discord and a complete lack of the principle that Owen had so impressively demonstrated at New Lanark, Scotland.

Whatever the reasons, and there were many, Joseph Smith, the founder of Mormonism, had had many bitter enemies from the day in 1830 when he startled the people at Palmyra, New York, by announcing a whole new body of revelation from the Almighty and mobs had driven him into hiding more than once. Smith attracted followers as well as enemies and Mormonism grew. At Kirtland, Ohio and Independence, Missouri people in surrounding communities reacted with violence. In spite of mobs Mormon missionary activity increased and more and more converts appeared. Smith became more positive and sweeping in his claims and plans in the Mormon capital at Nauvoo, Illinois, on the Mississippi. He made known his intention of taking over the government of the state in Springfield and ultimately establishing a Mormon regime in Washington. In Nauvoo he made what was probably his biggest mistake, his avowal of a revelation proclaiming polygamy. The old hate flamed more hotly than ever and Joseph and his brother Hyrum died at the hands of a mob in the old stone jail at Carthage. The jail is still there and the quiet little town of Nauvoo dreams on its high hill looking out over the wide bend of the river.

There are still a few Mormons in Nauvoo, descendants of those who stayed on after the westward migrants headed for Utah. They view themselves as the authentic chosen people and regard the Utah body as dissenters and renegades. Joseph Smith's house still stands, a museum of heavy early Victorian furniture with a good colonial piece here and there. Another old house is marked as the birthplace of John Browning, the inventor of the Browning automatic pistol. After the Young party had crossed the Mississippi on their long trek to their promised land, the Icarians appeared, one of the many communistic splinters scattered over the East and Midwest under the influence of the movements for social reform that flourished in the early nineteenth century. The Icarians left their mark on Nauvoo in the form of light graceful furniture, a vast improvement over the ugly bulbous pieces that the Mormons made.

In the turmoil of fears and wild suggestion that followed the killing of the Smiths there appeared the great leader, the statesman of Mormonism, Brigham Young. Young was in the East on a missionary tour, but he hurried back when he heard the tragic news. He was one of the twelve apostles in the Mormon organization and he had a shrewd mind. He soon reached the conclusion that the only hope for the faithful lay in leaving the United States and he would lead them. "Somewhere west," he told his people, they would find peace and the opportunity to live their own lives. Before they could begin to search and plan they must turn their backs on Nauvoo and endure the long agony of the trek across Iowa. The weather was generally bad and sometimes worse than that, food was scanty, the people along the way were unfriendly, fire and shelter were often lacking, but they won through to Council Bluffs where they were at least on the farthest verge of Iowa. Beyond were wide plains and then the mountains where they might find their safety. Here they picked up word of a sandy, salty desert and a great salt lake at the foot of the Wasatch Mountains. There were huge trees in the mountains and streams of sweet water. And these blessings were outside the United States, they thought. Here in the land of Deseret, as Young called it, they would build a republic of their own. (Deseret was a word coined by Smith in the Book of Mormon. The translation suggested for it was "honey bee.")

A trial trip was indicated and the tireless leader set about it without delay. They were already trail-hardened; the slow drag across Iowa from Nauvoo had taken a full year and many of the fainthearted had fallen by the wayside. Those who stuck were painfully acquainted with hunger and cold and every kind of privation. They knew the value of patience, and consciousness of the distrust and dislike of the Gentiles they saw along the way had welded them into a compactness that was like that of a veteran army.

Hard as the trip across Iowa had been it was not all hunger and cold. Mormons danced and sang wherever they were. Had not the ancient Israelites worshipped their stern God with song and with dance? So the shrewd Brigham Young encouraged these diversions as he was later to encourage the theater in the land of Deseret. On the drag across Iowa a Captain Pitt organized a band that played whenever there was a chance of a fee, eggs, vegetables, corn, a pail of honey, a ham or a few sides of bacon, sometimes even money, once twenty-five dollars and a good feed for the band. Beyond Council Bluffs on the way up the Platte the Mormons more than once took time to set up a ferry service for parties of less resourceful Gentiles bound for Oregon.

No stranger migration than this has been seen, fifteen or twenty thousand people on the move carrying all their worldly goods with them, strangers in a strange land yet somehow fitting themselves to the needs of the moment. Brigham preached self-reliance more often than trust in the Lord. On one occasion in the High Plains, the lack of water had driven the travelers to the point of desperation and the people murmured; surely the leader had only to ask the Lord for rain and it would be forthcoming. Brigham reproved them for their little faith. "I can't be running to the Lord all the time for every little thing. This is His way of testing you. If you stand fast in the faith He will send the rain in His own good time." Fortunately for the leader a day or two later abundant rain fell and the grumbling ceased.

It was early in April 1847 that Young led out the advance party that was to find the permanent home remote and secure, "somewhere outside the United States." The preparations for the journey into the unknown had been thorough, Brigham had seen to that. In that first party there were 73 wagons, 143 men, 3 women, and 2 children. Among the men were blacksmiths, cobblers, carpenters, wheelwrights, farriers; most of the men jacks of all trades. This was the age when "do-it-yourself" was a law of life. There were tools, spinning wheels, looms, anvils, whatever was needed to set up housekeeping in a remote wilderness.

Knowing the value of titles Young had appointed two Captains of Hundreds, five Captains of Fifties, fourteen Captains of Tens, but he kept in his own hands the power of final decision. He decided where to stop and when, in game country he chose the hunters to supply fresh meat, he would know when they had reached the final location. (The legend is that when that first party emerged from the hard struggle through the Wasatch and saw the wide sweep of the Salt Lake Valley Young struck his staff on the ground and declared "This is the place!") Services were held daily at which Young exhorted them to cease their quarrelsome ways and to abstain from conduct that would hamper the building of their Mormon commonwealth. Contrary to the custom of the day there must be no drinking or gambling. In the whole history of the westward movement there was no wagon train that moved with less friction or greater unity of purpose than did that led by Brigham Young. It is no wonder that William E. Seward, Lincoln's Secretary of State, called this man the greatest statesman of his time.

Large and important as it was the Mormon hegira was an isolated chapter at the time, a sideshow. Larger things were in the making. The Mexican war ending with the Treaty of

Guadeloupe-Hidalgo, February 2, 1848, changed many things, including the map of the west. Texas, New Mexico, and California were now a part of the United States and Brigham Young's hope of escaping from the country was a futile dream. But the Mormons had found their place where there were no neighbors but a few naked savages. They saw a barren sandy plain but there was water in the Wasatch Mountains. The first step was to bring the water to the thirsty sand and they set about this forthwith. Soon the desert began to blossom.

It is time to recapitulate these chapters of our national saga in terms of geographical area. The western boundaries of the Louisiana Purchase may have been vague — "as received by us from Spain—" but the list of states to be carved from that imperial domain is impressive. Count them over on a modern map: Louisiana, Arkansas, Missouri, Iowa, Minnesota, the Dakotas, Montana, Wyoming, Nebraska, and parts of Kansas, Oklahoma, and Colorado.

To complete the picture look at the states that came to us by the terms of the Treaty of Guadeloupe-Hidalgo ending the war with Mexico: New Mexico, Arizona, California, Utah, Nevada, and a slice of Colorado. The statesmen of that day little understood the dimensions of their real estate deals. The treaty with England ending the long wrangle over the northern boundary — Forty-nine North instead of "Fifty-four Forty or Fight" as the super-patriots had clamored in the election of 1846 — had brought into the national fold the present states of Washington, Oregon, and Idaho. In less than fifty years our continental map had been filled from sea to sea. It had taken two hundred years to get ready for it but the old dream of reaching the Western Ocean had been realized and in a big way.

It was the finding of gold in California that gave a totally new complexion and purpose to the long westward march. The trappers had wanted only beaver and the place for that was in the mountains; Whitman and his followers sought converts among the savages; covered wagon people wanted land for farms and homes in Oregon. Now it was California and the Land of Gold. The New York *Herald* of April 19, 1848, carried this random item: "I am credibly informed that a quantity of gold, worth in value $30.00, was picked up lately in the bed of a stream of the Sacramento." On October 6 of that year the S. S. *California* sailed from New York bound around the Horn for California carrying no passengers. When she reached San Francisco, February 28, 1849, the entire crew except the engineer jumped ship and headed for the gold fields. In that year forty-two thousand people made their way by land to California. There was a new urgency in the air and more than ever men sought a way west. Traffic over South Pass trebled and men began to think of the Overland Trail as the road to Eldorado and not merely a vague region.

Before the finding of gold there had been three main objectives for the westward travelers, Oregon, the Salt Lake basin, and California. Fort Hall was the junction, the point of decision between Oregon and California, and Oregon had been the choice for most of them. When word came that there was gold to be found in the Sacramento valley the choice of routes was thrown into wild confusion, especially beyond Fort Hall. More than one party blundered through Echo Canyon to wreck what remained of the Mormon hope of peace and a law of their own. There was a growing demand for some kind of regular service overland. Emigrants formed their own groups and Mormons were concerned only with their own particular destiny. The Argonauts demanded a more regular means than hanging about St. Joe in hope of catching a ride; hitch hiking from the Missouri to Sacramento was not an attractive idea. The need for regular mail service was growing with the increase of population in California. A split stick beside the trail might satisfy the budding Oregonians, but it was not a gold hunter's idea of a post office.

The answer to the growing demand was twofold, Overland stages and the Pony Express. Russell, Majors & Waddell provided the stages and the route chosen was of course South Pass. Russell and Majors were experienced freighters and the carrying of passengers was a normal development for them. The real genius of the Overland Trail was Ben Holladay who bought out the Russell, Majors & Waddell outfit. He had had experience supplying wagons and supplies for troops during the Mexican war, especially Kearny in his long march to California, from Santa Fe to San Diego. He knew men and horses and he chose both with care and wisdom. He also changed routes. At his direction South Pass was abandoned as offering little chance for local traffic and too much for raiding Indians and Denver, already outgrowing its original stature as a booming gold camp and assuming the airs of a real town, became the end of the first grand division of the through run to Placerville in California. There were now three main divisions, Atchison, Kansas to Denver, Denver to Salt Lake City, Salt Lake City to Placerville, each approximately six hundred miles long, each with a division superintendent. Each of these main divisions consisted of three smaller divisions, each approximately two hundred miles long with a division agent as boss.

Including the east and west terminals there were a hundred and fifty-three stations, one every twelve or fifteen miles, depending on the character of the country, small "swing" stations with extra horses waiting. About every fifty miles there was a "home" station and provision for meals and if needed beds of a sort, although as a rule passengers preferred to ride straight through.

An average run for both drivers and teams was two or three stages, twenty-five to fifty miles. At the height of its brief period of glory the Overland Stage had no less than a hundred and fifty drivers and four to six times that number of horses. The drivers were the best that could be found and were inordinately proud of their skill with the four- or six-horse teams that were used. When young Samuel Clemens came through on the Overland he found many men anxious to give him their various versions of the remark made by Hank Monk to Horace Greeley, probably another wild west invention. But Hank Monk was one of the crack drivers and Horace Greeley did ride the Overland. Fares were high, Atchison to Placerville $225.00. With the depreciation of the currency during the Civil War this skyrocketed to $525.00, but stages as a rule ran full.

A weird exception to the general rule of reliability and order among Overland employees was one Joseph A. Slade, agent of the Julesberg division. He was ordered to clean out a gang of thieves and cutthroats operating around Julesberg and in the process "cleaned out" the station agent Jules Beni for whom the station was named. Slade soon became a marked man because of his skill with a six-gun and a record of twenty-six killings to his credit, a considerable contribution to the cause of law and order. His too frequent quarrels and growing addiction to the bottle ended in his dismissal from the company. From Julesberg he drifted to Virginia City in Montana Territory, a flourishing gold camp where the local vigilantes presently put a permanent end to his career. It is recorded that this champion killer did not make a worthy end, groveling at the feet of his judges and begging for his life for his wife's sake.

Young Clemens en route to the Nevada camps with his brother Orrin reported that he sat next to the terrible Slade at breakfast and found him "the most gentlemanly appearing and affable officer in the Overland's service," for all his gruesome score. Later Clemens happened upon a little book by Prof. Thomas J. Dimsdale, *The Vigilantes of Montana; being a reliable account of the Capture, Trial and Execution of Henry Plummer's Road Agent Band*. From this classic Clemens quotes approvingly the reference to Slade: "From Fort Kearney, west, he was feared a good deal more than the Almighty." Clemens adds, "for compactness, simplicity, and vigor of expression, I will back that statement against anything in literature."

After Holladay's career with the Overland was ended by the opening of the railroad he looked about for other openings. He was a friend of Brigham Young, although no Mormon, and he knew his way about in Congress and in many state legislatures. He tried his hand at ocean freights along the California coast and wisely concluded that the coming of rails and steam meant the end of windjammers, even with steam to help. He took a whirl at railroad building in Oregon and was on his way to fortune when the panic of 1873 upset a lot of apple carts. Even so his contributions to the history of the west were large. He was a figure of legend while he was still alive. A young man wandering in the Holy Land was unimpressed by the story of Moses and the children of Israel and their forty years in the wilderness on their way to the Promised Land. "Ben Holladay," the doubter declared, "would have fetched them through in thirty-six hours."

The Pony Express was a brief and unimportant marginal note in our history that has acquired a lustre out of all proportion to its usefulness or durability. This was a drama, melodrama even, of men and horses that was irresistible. It grew out of a friendship between Senator William McKendrie Gwin of California and B. F. Ficklin, general superintendent of Russell, Majors & Waddell. Ficklin wished to add lustre to the already substantial reputation of the firm. Gwin was a Southerner, but he was also a Californian and saw a chance for political advancement in this plan for high speed communication from coast to coast. He introduced a bill in the Senate in 1855 but the issue of the day was slavery and the bill died in the Military Affairs committee. As time drew on to 1860 it became increasingly clear that the chance of a southern route to the coast, whether stage, freight wagon, or pony, had gone glimmering although John Butterfield and William Fargo were running a mail and freight route from Memphis and St. Louis to El Paso and on to California. For northern Californians such service was almost worse than none at all, making them dependent on southern sources in the event of war.

Now the Russell, Majors and Waddell firm stepped in in the person of William H. Russell. His partners were not too sure of the soundness of Russell's judgment but he was persuasive and Ficklin was persistent and the idea was sensational and so the partners came along and the date for the inauguration of the service was set for Tuesday, April 3, 1860, "at five o'clock p.m." A measure of the quality of these men can be gained by a look at the size and details of the organization. Before the first riders left Sacramento or the Missouri a hundred and ninety stations must be located where the four hundred and twenty horses necessary would be waiting and four hundred station men and helpers must be hired. The riders would average seventy-five miles at a stretch with ten miles to a horse, if there was no interference from Indians. They were carefully chosen, eighty of them, at a wage of a hundred to a hundred and fifty dollars a month. They were particularly proud of their ability to make a quick change from horse to horse and there were fervid accounts of the flying leap from the saddle as the horse made his last stride to the saddle of the new mount. The standard time for the change was two minutes and this was bettered many times. Only first class mail was carried and the postage rate was five dollars an ounce —

sometimes stated as a half ounce. The schedule from St. Joe to Placerville was ten days, and in good weather the run could be made in as little as seven days.

Legends began to gather before the last rider made his run. One favorite yarn, evidently emanating from the publicity manager of Buffalo Bill's Wild West Show, was that that picturesque character had been one of the best of them. Mr. Cody was fifteen years old at the time. Truly boys became men early in those days. To the riders "Pony Bob" Haslam was the hero. On one occasion Haslam rode a hundred and ninety miles in a single stretch when Indians raided stations. After nine hours he declared himself rested and ready to go again.

The first rider started from St. Joe early in the evening of April 3. Of course there was oratory; in that day of spellbinding it could hardly be otherwise. Mr. Jeff Thompson, mayor of St. Joe, was the inevitable speaker. This was his day and he made the most of it. Fortunately for posterity his words, some of them at least, have been preserved. His peroration is worth reading:

> The mail must go Hurled by flesh and blood across two thousand miles of desolate space — Fort Kearney, South Pass, Fort Bridger, Salt Lake City. Neither storms, fatigue, darkness or Indians, burning sands or snow must stop the precious bags. The mail must go!

It should cause no surprise to learn that the redoubtable Thompson appeared later as the probable original of Colonel Mulberry Sellers in Mark Twain and Charles Dudley Warner's "Gilded Age." They had both known him. Long after the Mayor's oratorical blessing the same sense of dedication was expressed in the inscription on the new general post office building in distant New York: "Neither snow nor rain nor heat nor gloom of night stays these carriers from the swift completion of their appointed rounds."

Waddell's contribution to the joint effort was an oath which all employees, and especially riders, were required to sign:

> I - - - - - hereby swear before the Great and Living God that during my engagement and while I am an employee of Russell, Majors & Waddell I will under no circumstances use profane language; that I will drink no intoxicating liquors, that I will not quarrel or fight with any other employee of the firm, and that in every respect I will conduct myself honestly, be faithful to my duties and so direct all my acts as to win the confidence of my employers. So help me God!

The Pony Express was a gallant experiment and more than one otherwise forgotten cluster of humanity lost in the deserts of Utah or Nevada can sustain its local pride by claiming to have been a station on the way. Sensational as it was there just weren't enough letters worth five dollars an ounce; furthermore the telegraph was pushing fast through the mountains and in less than two years the express riders' day was done, but it had lasted long enough to win an honorable mention in our history — also long enough to send Russell, Majors & Waddell into bankruptcy.

CHAPTER IX

Steam and Steel

B Y 1850 it was becoming clear to a good many reason-
able men that only a railroad would satisfy the growing
demand for adequate transportation from the Missouri to the
Pacific. In spite of criticism and ridicule the day of steam
and steel was coming steadily nearer. This apparent contradic-
tion is not unusual or incongruous, calling attention to the
growing possibility of the impossible. As the blood of the martyrs was the seed of the church, so the failures of the pioneers
clear the way for those who will not fail. Good politicians
know that it's better to be laughed at than ignored. That had
been the case with Robert Stephenson, the first man who had
made a teakettle on wheels sit up and get to work. When a
pompous member of Parliament asked him what would happen if a cow got on the track wise Robert gave laconic answer:
"It would be the waurse for the coo." It was the old struggle
between the new and uncertain and the slow but sure. But a
railroad across deserts and mountains? Could such a thing
be possible?

There were courageous dreamers who believed it could
be done, had believed it before a mile of railroad was operating
anywhere in the world. In 1819 one Robert Mills proposed a

steam road from the head of the Mississippi to the valley of the Columbia. Thirteen years later an anonymous writer in the *Emigrant* of Ann Arbor, Michigan, came forward with a plan for rails from New York to Oregon by way of the Great Lakes and the valley of the Platte. By that time there were a hundred and forty miles of railroad in the United States.

Dr. Hartwell Carver, grandson of Jonathan, an early explorer with an overactive imagination who had schemed to grab the credit for Robert Rogers' plan to find a northwest passage up the Missouri and the Platte and down the Columbia, besought Congress to authorize a railroad to Oregon based on a land grant. The gauge was to be eight or ten feet with rails laid on felt to lessen vibration, cars to be a hundred feet in length, with combined sleeping and dining facilities. Dr. Carver assured Congress that such a road would bring about "a kind of earthly millenium, and would be the means of uniting the whole world in one great church, a part of whose worship will be to praise God and bless the Oregon railroad."

William Gaylord Clark blossomed out in the *Knicker-bocker Magazine* with this presentation bouquet for the Pacific railroad: "The granite mountains will melt before the hand of enterprise; valleys will be raised, and the unwearying fire-steed will spout his hot, white breath where silence has reigned since the morning hymn of young creation was pealed over mountain, flood, and field."

The blue ribbon probably belongs to Capt. Albert Pike of Arkansas. In 1849 Capt. Pike proposed three lines from the Atlantic by way of Memphis, St. Louis, and Chicago respectively, the three joining hands at some point in the valley of the Missouri, to be agreed upon, the cost of the whole shebang to be borne by Uncle Sam. To the argument of cost he asserted: "If the old Shepherd Kings of Egypt could use the labor of half a million men and squander uncounted treasures and thousands of human lives to build those great Pyramids which 'doting with age have forgotten the names of their founders' which still stand in solitary majesty casting their broad shadows on the mighty Nile; for the sole purpose of serving as sepulchres for a King, an ibis, or a cat — great mountains of stone of no use to Egypt or the world; it would be strange indeed if a Republic of twenty million of freemen, richer than all the monarchies of Ormuz and of Ind, could not build a road which will pour the whole wealth of China and Hindustan and the islands of the Indian sea into its lap." The good captain wasn't so far wrong at that, but it didn't happen quite as he expected.

There were martyrs of course as well as heroes in those times. Colonel Low, a professor in St. Joseph's College in Bardstown, Kentucky, wrote a pamphlet advocating a railroad to the coast. The trustees of the college, using the pamphlet itself as their only evidence, fired the colonel on the ground of insanity. College trustees can do curious things at times.

Among the prophets with a faint touch of financial realism was Asa Whitney. Here was a shrewd Yankee born in North Groton, Massachusetts, who came up with a plan for financing a transcontinental railroad before even a mile of survey had been run west of the Mississippi. His idea was a grant of land thirty miles wide on each side of the line to be sold to settlers as the road was built. "Sensible" men scoffed at this as an impossible dream and showed that with due allowance for time to sell the land a hundred and seventy to three hundred and eighty years would be needed to translate dream into reality. Whitney lived to see transcontinental lines built and trains running, although he was forced to be content with a dairy route in the city of Washington.

John Plumbe of Iowa crusaded steadily for the railroad idea from 1836 to 1840. At a railroad meeting in 1847 he was hailed as the "Original Projector of the Great Oregon Railroads," although it was twenty years before such a thing came into being.

Benton of Missouri, advance agent of Manifest Destiny, had a transcontinental idea all his own. His prophetic eye glimpsed a turnpike built by federal funds from the Missouri to the Pacific and lined with army posts, "A road on which the farmer in his wagon or carriage, on horse or on foot, may travel without fear and without tax, with none to run over him or make him jump out of the way." Unfortunately for the senator our Destiny was not quite so Manifest as that.

The early railroads were patchwork affairs, locally financed, poorly built, stretching from "nowhere to nothing." There was no coherence of organization or intention. Before the Civil War something that was to be known as the New York Central System was vaguely apparent between Albany and Buffalo, but travelers over the route found themselves under the necessity of patronizing eleven different carriers following as many different schedules with separate stations often involving long walks or longer waits to make connections. It took several years and Cornelius Vanderbilt to knit these lines together and crown the whole with a line along the east bank of the Hudson tying New York City into the emerging system. Even so it took a long time to throw a bridge across the river at Albany. Until that came passengers were ferried over in rowboats or in winter were given permission to walk across on the ice.

There was wide variation in gauge from the narrowest of the narrow, sometimes as little as two feet, to the giants of five or even six feet. What was to become the controversial Erie began life as a six-footer and some of the small ones lasted well into the present century. Apparently a prime object was to discourage the exchange of traffic rather than to build it up. While this absurd practice continued local teamsters and freight-handlers made a good profit bridging the gaps. The standard gauge of four feet eight and a half inches was a heritage of imperial Rome. That was the length of the axles of the chariots that marked the Roman roads from the heart of the empire to Hadrian's wall. The British accepted this without question as part of the way things were, leaving the restless Yankees to learn their lesson by trial and error.

Politically and culturally the decade from 1850 to 1860 was a gloomy one. Bitterness between North and South was growing. In the North William Lloyd Garrison had made grim pronouncement that slavery was a sin and there could be no compromise with sin and in the South John C. Calhoun had made clear his doctrine of the perfect society resting on the slave with leisure for the cultivation of the finer arts of living by the master class. God had ordained that the negro be the hewer of wood and the drawer of water for all time and there were more than a few Northerners who agreed with him. The great leaders, Webster, Clay, Calhoun, John Quincy Adams, had stepped from the stage and their successors seemed puny dwarfs in a time calling for wise giants. There were fears and threats of war.

Gloomy as it was politically it was a decade of furious activity for the builders of railroads. When it opened rails had pushed west across the Alleghenies as far as Lake Michigan and south of the Ohio almost to the Gulf. In 1837, a year of panic disaster, the legislature of Illinois passed a bill for Internal Improvements, meaning railroads, to the disappointed wrath of the backers of canals. Both Abraham Lincoln and Stephen A. Douglas supported rails, in spite of the emotional wailing of the canal orators. As yet Chicago gave no signs of becoming a railroad center, or a center of anything except mosquitoes and malaria, but the thing was in the making. Before war seized the center of the stage the Mississippi had been bridged at Rock Island and Abraham Lincoln had won a case for the railroad that had built the bridge, later to be known as the Chicago, Rock Island, and Pacific. This case brought into sharp focus the growing rivalry between rail and water transport. A steamboat rammed a pier of the new railroad bridge across the Mississippi at Rock Island and promptly sued the railroad company for heavy damages on the ground of obstructing traffic. Rails won and the writing on the wall became clearer. Before Sumter was fired on there were thirty thousand miles of railroad east of the Mississippi, two-thirds of it north of the Ohio.

For all the speed of railroad growth in that time nobody knew much about the job, as was shown by the fumbling over gauges and schedules. Just for example, what time is it? That's a simple question that any schoolboy can answer, but schoolboys weren't making the schedules and the locomotive had changed the nature and dimensions of the problem of time. Before the day of the railroad time was what you wanted to make it. Men worked from "sun to sun" and if the day was cloudy the worker made his best guess and let it go at that. Sun time was supposed to be the correct time, with little regard to the fact that sun time varied with the variance of longitude. Each community suited itself and set its clock accordingly. As late as the late nineties "early candle-lighting time" was still being used for such things as the Wednesday evening prayer meeting. This was all very well for villagers and country people who lived by the sun but as railroads spread more and more people really needed to know what time it was. Even so the idea of standardizing time aroused violent opposition. Newspaper editors wrote violent diatribes against tampering with anything as old as time. Ministers attacked standard time as sacrilege. Railroads struggled to make schedules and fix connections in this hurlyburly of discordant clocks. Such distinctions as "local" time, "sun" time, "railroad" time were common. Before we laugh too loudly it might be well to remember the bitter feelings aroused over daylight saving time. At least one state, Connecticut, forbade the display of daylight time on any public clock, compelling the citizens of the Nutmeg State to bootleg daylight time. The term "God's time" did not die with the adoption of standard time zones in 1883.

Incidentally there were two benefactors of the human race who deserve to be remembered. The earlier one was C. F. Dowd, the head of the Temple Grove Seminary for Young Ladies at Saratoga Springs. Professor Dowd took time out from his academic duties to propose that chaos be turned into order by establishing time belts across the country. That was in 1873. Then in 1883 William Franklin Allen, secretary of the Time Convention, proposed time zones based on the 75th, 90th, 105th, and 120th, meridians and on November 18 of that year the plan went into effect. Now time was what the railroads said it was.

Then there was the matter of finance. That had seemed difficult enough when the projected line was only twenty or thirty miles long. Sometimes ambitious towns came across with the land for the right of way through the town or the primitive stations and yards. It was hard to convince a hesitant investor that there was profit to be found in a railroad. There were many communities and industries to be served, but weren't stagecoaches and canals safer and surer? Prejudice dies hard. If shortsighted capitalists hesitated to dig into their pockets to pay for a few shares of stock in the eight-mile pigmy from Billerica to Bedford, in congested Massachusetts, how would they feel about taking a chance on a railroad from the Missouri to the Pacific, eighteen hundred miles of it, and all through a wilderness that had no people or towns and probably never would have? This was no job for private capital. If the government needed such a road to haul troops and supplies to keep the Indians in order let the government pay for it.

In California the debate over railroads versus wagons was still more confused. When the war with Mexico ended the land of gold was in the Union but there were differences of opinion over the future of the state. For a brief time there was talk of an independent Republic of California. A flag was designed flaunting a hulking, arrogant grizzly. A few took this hope seriously, the fantastic John C. Fremont perhaps, but such ideas faded out with the discovery of gold. A new danger now presented itself, that of seizure by England. English ships were common along the coast and English men of war appeared during the war with Mexico, ostensibly for the protection of British citizens and interests.

After 1850 California seemed firmly in the Union but early in the Civil War the Mason-Slidell affair roused fresh rumors and suspicions. These two gentlemen were prominent Confederates on their way to England on a British ship which had been taken from under the British flag by a Union man of war. Wars have started over less provocation than this. Tempers flared in England and there was the usual loud talk. William E. Seward, Lincoln's Secretary of State, expressed himself publicly as in favor of standing pat, even at the risk of a break with England. If that happened what was to prevent the English from taking over the whole Pacific Coast at which they had cast envious eyes since the days of Drake? Fortunately the President, who had better sense than his whole cabinet, curtly assured his Secretary of State that one war at a time was quite enough. The Confederate emissaries were returned to the shelter of the British flag and due apology was offered and as promptly accepted. There was little mystery about the mission of Mason and Slidell, merely another futile attempt to secure recognition and aid from the British and French governments. As on so many other occasions foreign offices talked much but did little and the ice remained thin for some time. Privately British statesmen were hopeful that the war would bring about the downfall of the upstart Republic for which they had hoped ever since the Revolution. In France the tinsel and gilt emperor Louis Napoleon was secretly plotting an invasion of Mexico while the Union was fighting for its life. All that came of these extravagant dreams was the Austrian Archduke Maximilian, erstwhile Emperor of Mexico, facing a firing squad of Mexican soldiers. Ten years later Louis Napoleon fled to England to die in exile there.

In addition to the war scares and the prospect of British seizure there was much difference of opinion in California over the need for railroads. As elsewhere conflicting interests made themselves heard. Freighting companies were sending their lumbering wagons over the High Sierras and down to the growing market in the new Nevada mining camps. Stage lines talked with large vagueness about the impossibility of keeping a railroad open during the fierce winter storms at the high levels. Steamship lines running to the Isthmus joined in the chorus of warning. Even a group operating a line of boats bringing ice down from Sitka found a reason for declaring themselves in on this merry war. Just what their reason was has never been made clear.

It is interesting to note that the Nevada mines enjoyed mail service from Sacramento for a long time before rails came over the big hill. A Norwegian by the name of John A. "Snowshoe" Thompson was the carrier. Traveling on skis or snowshoes he set a surprising mark for regularity — two days down, three days up — for thirteen long winters. A tablet in his memory was set up in Carthay Center in Los Angeles, in 1926.

With such a discordant clamor of interest it is natural that general opinion should be confused and vague. One thing is sure, however, these men — and they were mostly men, wives and children would come later — felt themselves in the Union but not quite of it and they didn't like this uncertainty of status. Whatever the magnet that had drawn them to California, they looked back with longing to the homes from which they had come. Much as they liked the new country, they felt themselves a stranded people separated from the rest of the country by distance, time, and cost. They knew nothing about building railroads or running trains, but the belief grew that a railroad might be just the tie they needed to make them feel at home in this far land. By 1860 the new state had a population of 379,994, enough to count as an important unit.

Railroad building demands trained engineers, not the dramatic hero of the throttle but the more important plodder who runs the surveys, plots the curves, painfully figures the cost of cuts and fills, and placates the irate farmer through whose fields the line is to run. Since few people knew much about the building or operating of the newfangled roads the air was filled with plans for roads that never got beyond the talking stage. Many men called themselves engineers whose only qualification was their confidence in themselves, but two men appeared, both Yankees, who were to write their names indelibly on the roster of great builders. One of them was Grenville Mellon Dodge, son of a farmer near Danvers, Massachusetts, the other, Theodore Dehone Judah, son of an Episcopal minister in Bridgeport, Connecticut, later to be called "Crazy" Judah.

These two men were marked by fate for high responsibility in the most daring railroad dream yet conceived, nothing less than building a line across the High Plains, through the main range of the Rockies, across the dreary deserts of Utah and Nevada, and over the high passes of the Sierras into the land of gold. Dodge was to live to see the completion of the whole transcontinental system. Judah died young, before any of the first line had passed beyond the stage of a lunatic's dream, but he had shown the way to the "practical" men who saw only immediate profit where "Crazy" Judah had had a vision. The work of Dodge and Judah was both competitive and complementary. The stories of their lives are the halves of a single whole, the Pacific Railroad.

General Grenville M. Dodge, he really was a general and a good one, had his training at Norwich University in Vermont, graduating at the age of twenty, a military and a civil engineer, an unusual degree then but a significant one. His first job was with the infant Illinois Central Railroad as a surveyor in Peru, Illinois. This was in 1851. The young engineer found Peru an unexpectedly friendly place. Two of his classmates had preceded him there and were prepared to introduce him to the youthful society of the town. There were parties galore, barn dances, horseback rides, picnics, and long walks. In Peru he also found Miss Anne Brown whom he married in 1854.

Straight out of staid New England young Dodge found himself confronted by the Illinois landowner, a different breed of cat from the shrewd and usually peaceful Massachusetts farmer. Many men in Illinois still had faith in canals and took no stock in this agency of the devil roaring through their fields at twenty or even thirty miles an hour. Sometimes they were ready to back their prejudices with their dogs and shotguns. Surveyors must be diplomats as well as engineers. The

young man did well in both capacities. The Illinois Central
had large ambitions aiming at New Orleans as the ultimate
goal, challenging the mighty Mississippi, the great freight carrier to the Gulf. The state of Illinois was a useful backer,
granting the road a strip of land ten miles wide from Chicago
to Cairo at the junction of the Ohio with the Mississippi. Canals had received many acres in the past, but this was the first
case of rails as the beneficiaries of the state treasury. More
would be heard of land grants and soon.

Dodge crossed the river as an engineer for the Mississippi
& Missouri Railroad heading for Council Bluffs on the Missouri, where Lewis and Clark had sat in council with the Indians. Circumstances were shaping up for a longer jump that
men began to dream about. Crossing Iowa was easy for the
surveyors and the western terminus was reached in 1855.
Dodge told later about a talk he had with a lanky ex-Congress-
man from Springfield, Illinois named Lincoln. What they
said to each other in that brief talk has not been reported.
At the time the young engineer thought little of it except to
make a note in his diary, recording only "as the saying goes
he completely shelled my words," reminiscent of corn husk-
ing days on his father's farm in Massachusetts. There was talk
between them of the purchase of land at Council Bluffs, but
no evidence that it went beyond the talking stage. Railroads
and real estate were associated in men's minds then as for many
years to come.

Dodge and his surveyors had reached Council Bluffs easily
enough, but the building of the line must wait for the gathering of more capital than had yet appeared. Meanwhile Dodge
lingered on at this jumping-off place, which must have seemed
to him nowhere in particular. He freighted a little from the
Missouri to Denver, then much in the news as a growing gold
camp, later to be the metropolis of the Rockies. He studied

the flat, semi-arid plains and saw something of Indians. The first one he encountered tried to steal his horse while he was sleeping in the shade of a cottonwood. The sleeper waked in time and, as he noted in his diary, "hollered" so loud the horse thief ran for his life. Later Dodge found the same Indian serving in a Pawnee battalion under him in the campaign of 1865 against the Arapaho and Sioux in the Yellowstone country.

Before any westbound railroad could be built a larger war than all the Indian campaigns put together must be fought. In 1861 rebel batteries fired on a fort in Charleston harbor and that happened which had been foretold. The word for the day was War. Dodge the engineer became Dodge the fighter and stayed so for four years. As colonel of the 4th Iowa he took a wound at Pea Ridge and as brigadier a worse one in the fighting before Atlanta. He repaired railroads and built bridges. The bridge across the Chattahoochie, seven hundred and ten feet long and fourteen feet high in the center, took his gang three days to have ready for use. Grant praised him for this, a recognition that would do him no harm later. Between building jobs he fought and came out of the war a marked man. He had amply justified the military half of his degree from Norwich. Soon after the end was reached at Appomattox he was out of uniform and in civilian togs as chief engineer of what was to be the Union Pacific.

Meanwhile what of "Crazy" Judah? A graduate of Rensselaer Polytechnic Institute at Troy, New York, one of the pioneer engineering schools, he saw service briefly with New England railroads. Then he attracted wide attention by conceiving and building the Niagara Gorge Railroad, one of the daring achievements of the time. A message from the governor of the state called him to New York City for a talk with a C. L. Wilson from California who wanted a chief engineer for a nonexistent railroad from Sacramento to the placer mines of Dutch Flat to tap the market there. Judah didn't think much of California, but as Wilson talked the engineer began to warm up. Although the crowded East was obviously the place for railroads, perhaps here was the challenge he needed, a railroad adventure among high mountains and glistening snow fields. Who knew what might lie beyond? Certainly he did not, but it was a chance worth taking.

In 1854 he took ship for that wild land with his new wife Anna. Anna had been a belle in her home town in Massachusetts, hardly a likely candidate for such a fantastic venture, but she packed obediently and set forth for the long trip across the Isthmus and up the coast to the straggling California metropolis at the Golden Gate. For the next ten years she was to spend many lonely days wondering where her unpredictable husband was and what wild new scheme he was meditating. It was a safe bet that whatever he was up to was not what he had planned when he left her. To a less conventional wife it might have been an interesting, or even exciting life. Her only solace was sketching the mountain scenery about her, an occupation in which she had some skill.

Judah's first task was to build the line from Sacramento to the placer mines, only twenty-one miles with none but routine problems. Building through the gorge of Niagara was a heroic feat compared with this, for all the mountain landscape around him. Then another piece of work was handed him. Gold and silver had been found in large quantities in the Nevada desert and a new Eldorado was beckoning. Where there is treasure there men will go and where men are digging precious metals profit will be found. Could Judah find a way for loaded wagons over, through, or around the High Sierras to the turbulent camps in Nevada? He was opinionated and humorless, but he was also highly competent, for all his growing reputation as a raving lunatic. He found a practicable route, but why bother with horses when steam was waiting at the gate? His California backers were practical men and hence shortsighted so of course they slammed the door in the face of the locomotive. "Just like that crazy Judah," they said. "Never knows when he is well off." They were right there; he never did.

Because he never knew when he was licked he campaigned through central California arguing for the impossible. In September, 1859, he called together in San Francisco what he called a Pacific Railroad Convention. That kind of meeting was easy meat for Judah. He argued, opposed, resolved, did everything except sit still and the Convention voted to send him to Washington to talk to Congress and anyone else who would listen, even the President if he could venture so high. They didn't know how crazy this man was. He went to the White House as a matter of course and talked to the timid, helpless James Buchanan. In Congress he found an unexpected friend in John A. Logan from Illinois, "Black Jack," who was later to be one of the founders of the G.A.R. Logan wangled a room in the Capitol building where Judah set up his Railroad Museum, maps, plans, specifications, drawings by wife Anna. Always he talked.

The thing he wanted from Congress was approval of a railroad over the high passes and so to the Nevada mines — perhaps even beyond. Wagon roads were nonsense; rails could go wherever wagons could. Congress didn't seem to think he was mad. At least there were many visitors to his Museum and even some eloquence on the floor of the House in his behalf. A railroad to the Coast was no new thing to Congress. There had been several routes proposed, some of them involving prohibitive grades. Jefferson Davis had argued for a line from New Orleans to San Diego. This was probably the easiest to build and operate, but coming from a Southerner it had a taint of slavery. A northern route, somewhere near the line of the Overland stages, was equally suspect to Southerners. As early as 1852 a long report on the subject had been made to Congress, seven beautiful volumes containing much information about scenery, climate, flora and fauna, but not much about the topography of the country that would be helpful to a railroad builder. Judah saw the volumes and the pictures and made ironic comment on their useless beauty. In the end Congress voted to postpone the matter of a transcontinental railroad to a later session. Slavery held the center of the stage. Judah still undefeated went back to California and turned in his expense account, $40.00 for printing and circulars for a trip that had cost him twenty-five hundred.

Back in California he disappeared in the mountains in search of a practicable route through. He stayed at the high levels so long that the early snows caught him and he and his companions had to fight their way down from the heights to Dutch Flat, but he had found the way he wanted. In Dr. Strong's drugstore in that mining camp he spread a sheet of paper on the counter and wrote the "Articles of Association of the Central Pacific Railroad of California" and sold a bunch of stock to the druggist — the not so crazy Judah.

CHAPTER X

California's Big Four

WHEN Judah wrote the Articles of Association on that drugstore counter in Dutch Flat the Central Pacific Railroad was launched. Judah at least knew what he was doing; in his mind there was no room for doubt, but he knew that something more than Articles of Association was needed, money in a word, much more than he and the stout-hearted Dr. Strong could muster. Sacramento was the place to try for it. Businessmen there were making money fast and would be prompt to seize this glittering opportunity. He brought a small group together in a hall over the hardware store of Huntington & Hopkins and told them his story. There were four men of at least local importance in that meeting, Leland Stanford, groceryman, Collis P. Huntington and Mark Hopkins, hardware merchants and owners of the building in which they were meeting, and Charles Crocker, drygoods merchant. Destiny had marked these men for fame but they hadn't heard about it yet.

These were the Big Four of California legend, praised by many, damned by many others. Viewed in perspective they were a queerly assorted quartette. Look at them as they pass in review out of the fog of controversy that never quite clears.

112

All four were born in New York or New England, knowing hard work and narrow circumstances in youth, inured to privation. All had come to California for the same reason, as traders not as miners, although it was rumored that Huntington did try mining — for one day only. Others might bet their lives on the chance of a strike in the next pan or on another hillside or streambed. They would sell goods to these gamblers and take whatever profit the market would permit. Charge as much as the traffic would bear was to be the watchword of their lives. The diggers alternated between high hope and bleak disappointment. The diggers took the gold dust or the small nuggets of the miners with each passing day. Tomorrow would be like today. When the mines played out, as mines always do, there would be other buyers somewhere else and more profit. Gold is where you find it, trading is to be found wherever men are working and spending.

Of the four Hopkins was the oldest. Born in 1813 he was forty-nine years old when he appeared in the meeting over the hardware store in Sacramento. He was a rare bird in the turbulent aviary of a California gold camp. In manner he was genial, tolerant, fatherly, as his appellation of "Uncle" Mark indicated. Appearances are sometimes deceptive. Under his gentle exterior there was iron in "Uncle" Mark and a hard intolerance. His great detestation was waste. As the keeper of the books of account and the counter of pennies, he saved scraps of paper, to the amusement of the casual young clerks over whom he ruled. He imposed a harsh regimen on these gay youngsters, early to bed and early to rise, no gambling or consorting with the blowsy women with whom the camps were filled. He would sell goods to these ladies, but he would not let them come through the chaste doors of Huntington & Hopkins. Let them send a messenger.

He ate sparingly, little meat, and he neither smoked nor drank at a time and in a place where most men did both with considerable enthusiasm. Vegetables were hard to find and the Chinese growers were shrewd judges of market values and Hopkins resented the high prices they set. It was perfectly proper for Huntington & Hopkins to charge what the traffic would bear, but the rule was not intended to work in reverse. The genial "Uncle" Mark bought a strip of rich alluvial land in the Sacramento River bottom and grew his own vegetables. The fertile soil gave him more than he needed and he sold the surplus, of course at a top price. Late in life he yielded grudgingly to his wife's urging and built a showy home on Nob Hill in San Francisco as evidence of his success, but he never lived in it. Today a glittering hotel stands high on the site of his futile palace and golden lads and lassies dine and dance there in the Top of the Mark.

Collis Potter Huntington was the Yankee trader pure and simple. On his first trip to California he was delayed for three months at the Isthmus waiting for a ship to take him the rest of the way. Other passengers fretted and drank and gambled and ran temperatures, but young Huntington traded, walking tirelessly through the tropical jungle, crossing the Isthmus on foot more than twenty times, finding articles to buy or sell in the most unlikely places. When the long wait ended the twelve hundred dollars with which he had left New York had become five thousand. He was a big man with a powerful body and a keen nose for a bargain. He was without sentiment and he was immune to criticism. He made no speeches and he sought no publicity. In his simple code the only virtue greater than that of making money was saving it. Opposition he attacked head on, wasting no time in tactical maneuver.

He was abundantly hated and feared, but neither hate nor fear disturbed him. Arthur McEwen, a writer for Hearst newspapers, saw him on his last visit to California and set him down as "a hard, cheery old man with no more soul than a shark." An unnamed observer described him as "scrupulously dishonest." The old man ignored praise and blame alike.

Nevertheless there was another side to Huntington. In his autobiography "Up from Slavery" Booker Washington tells of going to see him on behalf of his Tuskegee Institute. Huntington grimly handed out two dollars. There is no record of a later meeting but a few months before the railroad king's death he sent Washington a check for $50,000. Another Huntington benefaction, albeit an indirect one, was the Huntington Library at San Marino on the edge of Pasadena in California. This is one of the great institutions of the world, a boon to scholars everywhere. It was made possible through the interest and generosity of Henry Edwards Huntington, nephew of Collis and heir to the bulk of his huge fortune. The Huntington Hospital, also in Pasadena, was another result of Huntington millions coming by the same roundabout route.

Of Charles Crocker there is less to be said. Here was another man of granite endurance. Chance took him from behind a counter measuring out dress goods by the yard and set him to hiring graders and track-layers by the thousands. He seemed tireless but there were occasional periods of lethargy when he hid away in his work car, seeing no one, saying nothing. He knew short stretches of depression when he was ready to sell out his interest in the railroad for a clean shirt and go back to measuring dress goods. Most of the time he was broke but fighting.

Crocker's greatest contribution was the tapping of a new supply of labor, the Chinese. The day of the Argonauts was past and the easy digging and washing of Dutch Flat were things of yesterday, but the men who came from the East by boat or stage still dreamed of quick fortunes and swinging pick and shovel was obviously not the way to wealth. Crocker complained that the men he hired worked only long enough to get the money for the stage fare over the Sierras to the new Eldorado in Nevada. If a railroad was to be built it must be done by hand labor. The only construction machinery was small scoop scrapers with horses, or more likely mules, for the motive power. Ties were laid by hand and rails spiked down with sledges swung by human arms.

The gold camps had known Chinese labor but mostly as laundrymen or peddlers of food to the hopeful diggers. Why not give them a try as pick and shovel men? They couldn't be worse than the slippery white workers. It was the Chinese who took the Central Pacific over the top of the Sierras. Crocker hired two thousand of them in the first six months, six thousand in all. They came by the shipload mostly from Canton and they worked. Construction camps became surprisingly orderly and clean. They worked long hours, provided their own food, saved their pay, and if they gambled it was with each other. They soon learned all they needed to know about drilling and blasting. Near the top of the range there was a stretch where the road must be cut along the face of a sheer granite cliff, Cape Horn the survey gangs called it. Here Chinese powdermen were swung down from the top on long ropes to drill the holes and set the charges. When East and West met at Promontory Point the Chinese were still there swinging pick and shovel. The Irish of the Union Pacific gangs were proud of their prowess in grading and track-laying and thought little of the quaint Chinese. So great was the fervor to win this transcontinental race that the two lines overlapped for many miles — more than two hundred was one claim — so that competing gangs worked side by side. Once the veterans from the East set off blasts that showered the others with stones. The Chinese fought back with blasts of their own and the Union

Pacific men were more than willing to call it quits. Crocker's experiment was fully justified.

Crocker also built a palace on Nob Hill but he lived in his. There was never any doubt in his mind about the name of the man who built the Central Pacific; it was Charlie Crocker.

Leland Stanford, the fourth of the Big Four, is more difficult to place. Huntington was the money-raiser and the maker of contracts, Hopkins kept the books — and the money when there was any — and Crocker saw to the labor force. What did Stanford do? To begin with he had a strong affinity for the spotlight, a useful qualification for a career in politics. Stanford was governor for a term, then senator for twenty years. Governor was the title he preferred; it was there that he first tasted the sweets of political power, but a senator was a useful article to have in the house when railroads were in the making. Stanford was useful. He made many speeches; his slow, ponderous delivery, reading always from a prepared manuscript, impressed his hearers as the utterances of a wise and careful man who could be trusted. He seldom said anything much, which passed for prudence and sincerity. He had many admirers among newspaper writers whom he was careful to cultivate, further proof of his wisdom. His friends heaped extravagant praise on him, comparing him with Christ, Confucius, Caesar, Alexander the Great, Napoleon, John Stuart Mill. The reason for adding the sensitive, shy Mill to this glittering galaxy remains a mystery. One Stanford booster summed up the argument; Leland and not Lorenzo should be called the Magnificent, the greatest man who ever lived. Huntington called him "a damned old fool."

Stanford loved lavish display, as his houses, horses, ranches, vineyards, finally his university, Leland Stanford Junior University on his home ranch at Palo Alto, a memorial to his only son who died young, all show. This last was an unexpected human touch, the only reminder of Leland Stanford that remains.

There is a legend, a rumor, an echo, floating about in the atmosphere of the Harvard Yard, that belongs in the category of things that should be true whether they are or not. According to this faint whisper two names were brought to the desk of President Eliot of Harvard on a day in the late eighties. The president turned to his secretary with a question: "Do we know a Mr. and Mrs. Stanford of California?" The secretary whose memory was a storehouse of names and faces, made answer: "No, Mr. Eliot, we do not." Nevertheless the callers were admitted, an old couple simply dressed in the style of a slightly earlier day. The man went at once to the point. "Mr. Eliot, how much would it cost to replace Harvard University, lock, stock, and barrel?" College presidents are asked many curious questions, but this was something new even for Eliot. He looked out the window, drummed on his desk top, made the usual gestures of a man stalling for time. He explained that many things went to the making of a university that were more important than money. The old man nodded. "Yes, of course. But give us your best estimate." Then Eliot took a chance and named a substantial amount, perhaps thirty or forty million. The couple looked at each other and the old man nodded. "I think we can do it, Mother." Thus, says the legend, was Leland Stanford Junior University founded.

These men of the Big Four have been much praised and much condemned. They were great builders, courageous, risking everything to make their dream come true. They were greedy pirates, without scruple or mercy, willing to rob widows and orphans to fill their own pockets. Both verdicts are half-truths but less than the whole truth. Their business morals were those of the time, even better than some. The code of the day allowed dog to eat dog, and by prevailing standards these were good dogs. Their understanding and courage grew as they worked and they built a great memorial to themselves.

It was crazy Judah who followed a clear vision and took the major risks with open eyes. He tempted, taunted, tricked these four to the achievement of such fame and fortune as they had never dared dream of. What became of him? He followed his dream to the end. He was one of four men who became the first passengers over a California railroad, a flat car painfully pushed for a hundred yards over rickety rails in Sacramento. He saw the first locomotive landed in San Francisco, a fifteen tonner; with two flat cars it became the first train to reach railhead at Placerville. Unfortunately the placer deposits were petering out and the rails became streaks of rust. He made another trip to Washington to lobby for his perennial Pacific railroad bill. When his persistence was rewarded by the passage of the bill he wired to Sacramento: "We have drawn the elephant. Now let us see if we can harness him up." Even this achievement did not convince the businessmen in Sacramento. They paid him a hundred thousand dollars for his interest and to get rid of him, and he took ship for New York for the last time. In Panama he picked up a yellow fever germ that killed him soon after his arrival in New York, November 2, 1863. He was thirty-seven years old. Sixty years later employees of the Central Pacific took up a collection for a memorial to the dreamer which stands in the plaza before the station in Sacramento.

CHAPTER XI

Congress Acts

T HE ADMINISTRATION in Washington was hard put to it to find the money for fighting the war. Now it was being pressed to back a railroad to the Pacific. There was no doubt that California must be held in the Union and a Pacific railroad would help to do that. How could Washington achieve these two impossibles? The answer was land, nearly two thousand miles of it from the Missouri River to the Western Ocean. The Act of 1862 and the later Act of 1864 stipulated that the builders of the line should receive ten alternate sections on each side of the right of way for every mile of track built and approved, 6,400 acres per mile.

In addition the government agreed to guarantee bond issues as the completed work was approved at the rate of $16,000 per mile on level ground, rising to $32,000 per mile in broken country and to $48,000 per mile of track through the mountains. For bonds so guaranteed the government would hold a mortgage on the line and its equipment. Washington had heard of the dealings of the state of Illinois with the Illinois Central, but who would buy the flat, dry lands of the West? As well speculate on real estate in the Sahara. There were other objections. Advocates of States Rights shouted that the domain of the separate states was being invaded, always a handy argument for a needy politician in search of an issue.

In spite of doubts and opposition the same year that saw the first Pacific Railways Act saw the Homestead Bill signed by President Lincoln. Ever since the time of Alexander Hamilton, Uncle Sam had been trying to sell his land. After many experiments the lawmakers had settled on a price of a dollar and a quarter an acre, but even at that most years saw the government land office operating at a loss. Now it was proposed to give the land away, a hundred and sixty acres to any citizen, man or woman, who would agree to live on the land five years and make "improvements." Immigrants who had filed their "first papers" for naturalization had the same privilege. Uncle Sam was backing the colossal railroad project with land and government guarantees of railroad bonds. Now the genial uncle was undertaking to put families on the land who would in time become customers of the railroad. And it worked, to the confounding of the skeptics.

Nebraska illustrates the effectiveness of the homestead plan. The U. S. Census reports for 1850 show only zeros for Nebraska, then a Territory, although there were certainly some squatters there. In 1860 there were 28,841, not including Indians. Ten years later, the decade of Pacific railroad building, there were 122,993, and the railroad was less than a year old. By 1890 the state held 1,062,656. Here were customers for the railroad soon to be numbered in the millions, although not always happy ones. There were charges that the timing of the railroad and homestead acts, almost the same month, was proof of a conspiracy. If this was a plot it was a successful one.

As homesteaders pushed west they found themselves on the edge of the Nebraska sandhills and the short grass country of western Kansas lately the grazing ground of the endless herds of buffalo and Texas longhorns just off the long drive up from near the Rio Grande. This was the great American Desert. Zebulon Pike, on his way to the peak that bears his name, crossed it and remarked approvingly that here was a barrier "placed by Providence to keep the American people from a thin diffusion and ruin." Now fifty years later Uncle Sam was helping his children to break the barrier.

To tell the story of the building of the first transcontinental railroad is to ride two horses which seem often to be traveling in opposite directions. Consider the terms of the Pacific Railways Act passed by Congress in 1862. Part of this act seems plain enough. The incorporators of the Union Pacific Railroad Company are authorized and "empowered to lay out, locate, construct, finish, maintain, and enjoy a continuous railroad and telegraph from a point on the hundredth meridian of longitude west from Greenwich, between the south margin of the valley of the Republican River and the north margin of the valley of the Platte River," as far as the boundary between Nevada and California. Then the act goes on to authorize the Central Pacific Railroad Company of California to build to the eastern boundary of California. Nothing could be simpler than that, but there is a joker. The said Central Pacific Railroad is also authorized to keep right on east "through the Territories of the United States to the Missouri River . . . . . . until said roads shall meet and connect." The only equal to this charming verbiage in our history is that of King James fixing the boundaries of the colony of Virginia in the second charter wherein he identified the sidelines of the extension granted as running "west and northwest to the Western Ocean," a puzzling direction to ordinary surveyors. In neither case did the double talk do serious harm. There is a logic of circumstance that overrides the logic of lawyers and statesmen.

Congressmen in 1862 may not have been overburdened with knowledge of either railroad building or the geography of the remote West, but their intent is clear. Two horses approaching each other from opposite directions on the same line are almost bound to "meet and connect" somewhere, or words are meaningless. Only careful planning can prevent it, although the exact point of contact may be anywhere between California and the Missouri River. That much he who runs may read.

We have seen that, thanks to Judah, California got the jump on the East in setting to work. However unwilling the Big Four may have been to follow the pointing finger of Judah even as far as the Nevada line, surveys had been made and rails laid heading toward the summit of the Sierras.

The Pacific Railways Acts had settled one or two points. A railway was to be built and with government aid in land grants and guarantees of bonds; furthermore now that the South had declared itself out of the Union and was at war to make that declaration good, there was no longer need to consider the fears of the friends of slavery. The road could be built where the North wanted it and from the Missouri to the Pacific Coast roughly following the trail marked out by Mormons, Argonauts, and covered wagon people bound for Oregon. A railroad would ultimately be built along the southern boundary as Jefferson Davis had suggested, but the time for that was not yet.

It is one thing to pass a law, quite another to set it to work. Two years earlier Judah had secured the passage through the California legislature of an act incorporating the Central Pacific Railroad of California and had made a start in construction from Sacramento up to Dutch Flat. Judah at least was sure that he had found a practicable route over the Sierras to the Nevada desert and beyond, but he was careful to say

nothing about the "beyond." The Acts of 1862 had also provided for a line westward from a vague point on the hundredth
meridian to the western boundary of Nevada and for another,
the Central Pacific of California — already incorporated under California law — to build eastward across California.

The fixing of the start of the Union Pacific end of the
enterprise "at a point on the hundredth meridian west of
Greenwich" was another kind of talk, blind rather than double. The hundredth meridian crosses Nebraska nearly two hundred and fifty miles west of Omaha and Council Bluffs; the
Mississippi and Missouri Railroad stood poised at Council Bluffs
and that seemed the logical place for the jumpoff of the new
line. Three other points were competing for the honor of being the eastern end: St. Louis, Kansas City, and Topeka. Perhaps Congressional eyesight was better than it seemed.   If
other points wanted to get in on the transcontinental game let
them build their own roads to the meridianal starting place.
Topeka was thrusting out a feeble antenna in that direction
called the Topeka, Pawnee & Western. The T.,P.&W. never
made it. St. Louis and Kansas City made other arrangements
and Omaha became the place where the Union Pacific began.

Ground had been broken more than two years prior to
the arrival of Dodge in 1866 to take charge as chief engineer,
but not a foot of grade had been built. In the ground-breaking
ceremony a man named George Francis Train appeared and
made a speech. Train was an eccentric individual whose chief
activity seemed to be the making of speeches. He painted the
future of this western land in glowing colors and announced
his intention of building a town or two just to show how it
should be done.

He was a fantastic product of that turbulent time, not
financier, builder, nor engineer. His active life began at the age
of fifteen when he demanded and secured a position with Enoch

Train, a distant relative, head of a prosperous shipping business in Boston. Soon he was representing himself as an important figure in the firm rivaling even Cousin Enoch. One of his larger claims was that he gave the order to Donald McKay for building the *Flying Cloud,* greatest of the clipper ships. Then he moved to Australia where he developed a shipping business of his own, but the land Down Under could not hold him long. His restless feet took him to Europe and the Orient. At one time he appeared as an associate of Queen Maria Cristina of Spain, then he shifted to Ohio for a brief try at building the Atlantic & Great Western Railroad. Everywhere he went he made speeches, mostly about himself; he nominated himself for President of the United States, and at the time of the noisy argument over the sins and sorrows of Tilton and Henry Ward Beecher he spent some months in the Ludlow Street jail on a charge of publishing obscene matter. In the closing years of his life he was a lodger in the Mills Hotel in New York and spent hours talking with children at play in parks and streets. His speech at the ground-breaking ceremony of the Union Pacific was in keeping with his other exploits.

The problem of financing an enterprise so huge and daring as a transcontinental railroad was a prickly one at the best. In the case of the Union Pacific, driving through savage empty country most of the way, with scant water, forests, rock, hostile Indians; building only in the hope of traffic to come, money was a daily headache: a draft on an uncertain future. Government was giving land subsidies and guarantees of bonds, but they must be earned by sections completed and approved by the government inspectors. Land sales were far in the future, glittering prospects though they were. For all the grandiloquent prophesies of the millions of private capital that would be poured into the enterprise once the work was undertaken, private capitalists remained coy. Hopes and large prophesies will not pay wages and feed hungry workers or provide the rails and ties with which railroads are built. Out of this desperate need grew the most disreputable chapter in our whole railroad history, that which deals with the Credit Mobilier, a loathsome but almost inevitable expedient. Working capital must be found somewhere if subsidies were to be earned.

The organization of the railroad company was awkwardly planned for the building of the road. The president was General Dix, a dignified old gentleman without knowledge or experience of railroad construction or operation or the raising of money. Those mundane affairs were in the hands of Vice-President Thomas Clark Durant, a hard driving, plausible, devious promoter. A comparison of Durant's office in New York was that of C. P. Huntington, the money raiser for the Central Pacific, was revealing. Huntington's office was scantily furnished, bare of ornamentation, scarcely likely to impress a man who liked lots of frosting on his cake. Durant's office was large, richly furnished, adorned with flowers and cages of tropical birds — plenty of frosting.

The origin of Credit Mobilier is somewhat mysterious. In 1859 the legislature of Pennsylvania voted a charter to something called the Pennsylvania Fiscal Agency. Its purposes were obscure but its powers were large, as the future was soon to show. In March 1864, Vice-President Durant bought the charter of this vague entity and changed its name to the Credit Mobilier of America. George Francis Train contributed the new title, exhibiting some knowledge of the Credit Foncier of France, where dubious methods of raising money were much in vogue. Soon its technique of operation began to appear. Credit Mobilier bought up all the outstanding stock of the Union Pacific it could lay its hands on and reissued it to the stockholders of the Credit Mobilier, making the fiscal agency identical with the railroad company with the important difference that Credit Mobilier now began to make contracts for the building of the railroad, promising large profits.

In the process of getting Credit Mobilier under way shares of stock in the hybrid enterprise were distributed "where they would do the most good," including influential members of Congress of course. Now the names of two New Englanders began to appear in the plot, the Ames brothers, Oakes and Oliver, shovel makers in Easton, Massachusetts. Ames shovels were famous wherever men were digging in the dirt. Oakes was the important man in this firm, a figure of wide influence in New England finance, but Oliver, as a member of Congress, was not to be ignored. In the inevitable exposure and resultant investigation the Ames brothers were the targets of much of the criticism. Through most of the active period of investigation and exposure they were widely condemned as deliberate swindlers.

Time has brought clearer understanding and more just verdicts, and a granite monument on Sherman summit in Wyoming pays deserved tribute to the brothers. It seems now with a perspective of nearly a century on the whole shabby story that the shovel makers were quite willing to take a fat profit in dividends on their Credit Mobilier stock, but their interest did not stop there, as did Durant's. They were really concerned with building the railroad and Oakes assumed personal responsibility for investments in U.P. stock made by friends and associates, estimated by some as high as $47,000,000. He died believing himself a disgraced bankrupt, but his congressional brother was ultimately cleared of the censure that the House had voted against him.

Durant's attitude was in sharp contrast to that of the Ames brothers. He was the promoter pure and simple, seeing only a chance to take an unholy profit out of the construction shenanigans, sometimes close to a thousand per cent. Durant had no faith in the future of the railroad. Records show that on February 26, 1870, he held 36,522 shares of railroad stock gained through the manipulations of Credit Mobilier; two years later his holding of U.P. stock was only four shares. In 1872 Ames brothers and associates held a total of over 38,500 shares of U.P. stock.

It is difficult to unravel the mass of historical and statistical evidence accumulated about the charges, denials, exposures and claims of that time. Ethical standards in the business world a hundred years ago were anything but high. In dealing with the government it was generally assumed that charges would be padded to insure a fat margin of profit. How did Credit Mobilier operate? In essence it was very simple: Credit Mobilier financed the building of the road, providing material, paying wages, making contracts, in general acting as a construction corporation of course charging the railroad the full price for the material and services supplied. How much did Credit Mobilier take? There have been many guesses, some even of an amount greater than the actual total cost of the road with the water squeezed out. The involved character of the relationship of construction corporation and railroad is so bewildering that a clear cut answer seems impossible to find. On one occasion John M. S. Williams, a director, was asked if the road cost the railroad company more than it did Credit Mobilier. In his reply to the apparently plain question the witness achieved a masterpiece of verbal jugglery: "It depends upon how you look at it," he said. "If your right hand pocket had more money than your left and you took some from your right and put it in your left you would be neither richer nor poorer."

A single example will serve to illustrate the method in operation. An unknown man named Hoxie was awarded the contract for building the first hundred miles of grade west from Omaha. Hoxie at once assigned the contract to T. C. Durant, vice-president of the railroad, Cornelius Bushnell, C. A. Lombard, H. S. McComb, and H. W. Gray. The first four were directors of the railroad, Gray, a large stockholder. It was agreed that the contractors should receive the first government subsidy and land grant bonds to be issued when the first section was completed and approved by the government inspectors, thus insuring prompt payment and immediate profit. Quick profit was of the essence of the arrangement.

Peter A. Dey, chief engineer, old boss of Grenville M. Dodge on the Mississippi & Missouri job, had estimated the cost of the first hundred miles at $30,000 a mile and of the second hundred $27,000. Dey was a capable engineer and an honest man. Vice-President Durant instructed him to increase his estimate to $60,000 a mile in order to provide a wider grade and a longer radius for the curves. The estimate was raised, but the proposed changes in grade and curves were somehow overlooked. Dey promptly resigned, saying: "I do not approve of the contract made with Mr. Hoxie for building the first hundred miles from Omaha west and I do not care to have my name so connected with the railroad that I shall appear to endorse this contract."

The resignation of the chief engineer, which took place in 1864, seems to have had little effect on the progress of the work, which wasn't progressing. The war had entered its last stage; Union troops were pounding away at the Confederate defenses of Petersburg and public interest in the building of a transcontinental railroad was slight. The money that had been accumulated in the railroad treasury was spent in a pretentious ground-breaking ceremony in Omaha. In Washington all eyes were fixed on the duel between Grant and Lee. Orville H. Browning, who was Lincoln's Secretary of the Interior, might have been expected to show some interest in rails but he was more concerned that nothing should be done to disturb the Indians and had little faith in such a harebrained project as a railroad to California.

In an article in the *North American Review* of January 1869, Charles Francis Adams, an authority on corporate conduct and misconduct whose analysis of Erie Railroad trickery is still a classic, sums it up thus: "Who then constitute the Credit Mobilier? It is but another name for the Pacific Railroad Ring. The members of it are in Congress; they are trustees for the bondholders, they are stockholders, they are contractors. In Congress they vote the subsidies; in New York they receive them, on the plains they spend them, and in the Credit Mobilier they divide them; as stockholders they own the road, as mortgagees they have a lien on it, as directors they contract for its construction, and as members of the Credit Mobilier they build it."

It has been argued in defense of Credit Mobilier that this kind of financial manipulation was common, necessary in fact if working capital was to be secured. A similar method was used in California by the Big Four, known first as the Contract and Finance Company, later as the Western Development Company. It was war time and money was "tight," interest rates in California running as high as 2 per cent a month. Here as in the East the insiders, the Big Four, saw to it that the fattest contracts came to themselves, but thanks to Judah, the Californians found themselves actually engaged in building a railroad and under circumstances of considerable difficulty.

Eastern bankers naturally saw little hope for a transcontinental railroad. Where would passengers or freight be found in that savage, barren country? A group of cautious inquirers asked Huntington if he would guarantee the interest on Central Pacific bonds for the next ten years. Blunt, hard-faced Huntington promptly agreed, saying: "I will guarantee them because if the Central Pacific ever stops short of completion C. P. Huntington will be so broke that you will never waste any time picking up the pieces."

Another time a banker in New York threatened to sell the Union Pacific stock that Dodge had put up as collateral for a loan. Dodge appealed to Huntington as an authority on New York banking ways. "Tell him to go ahead and sell you out," said Huntington. "Tell him when he's through with you to try selling me out." The tough old man knew only too well that the market for Union Pacific stock was nonexistent.

For all the charges, exposures, claims, and counterclaims only a few things concern us now. The road was built and well built; no scandal has ever touched Dodge or the men directly associated with him. Later engineers have made changes in grade or curve as trains grew longer and heavier, but with no doubt thrown on the soundness of the original location and construction. Interesting light is thrown on the effectiveness of government grants and subsidies by a report from the General Land Office in 1943. Total land grants to all railroads in acres, 131,350,534; total miles built, 18,138; total of government loans for railroads, $64,623,512; total paid back by 1898-99, principal, $63,623,512; interest, $104,722,978. On some of the land grant railroads the money received from the sale of the subsidy lands was almost equal to the original cost of construction.

The worst feature was the identification or confusion of railroad and construction companies, an irresistible invitation for the padding of accounts and the multiplying of charges. Large profits were taken out of construction long before the railroad had had a chance to earn a dollar, a distinctly unhealthy state of affairs, the blame for which can be laid directly at the door of Thomas C. Durant. In the midst of so much rascality it was a marvel that the road was put through so rapidly and with such honest engineering and construction work.

A government inspector once asked Colonel Silas Seymour, a Union Pacific engineer, to define the term, "a first class road." Seymour's reply was quick and to the point. "A first class road is a first class road." And he was right. To add detail would have multiplied confusion. A story of Lincoln come to mind. The lanky Illinois lawyer was asked how long a man's legs should be. His answer was prompt and blightingly responsive: "Long enough to reach from his body to the ground."

CHAPTER XII

The Dirt Begins to Fly

THE ONE man who could be counted on to make the dirt begin to fly on the right of way, Grenville M. Dodge, was still in uniform, but there were signs that his mind was turning back to railroad building. He had been summoned to the White House not long before for a talk with Lincoln, and not about the war. The sad-eyed president had not forgotten that earlier talk with the young engineer. It is interesting to remember that when Dodge did come back to the western country it was a result of an understanding with T. C. Durant who had called on Dey for a bigger estimate of costs in order that a better grade might be built. He now assured Dodge of a completely free hand, a promise which of course was soon forgotten. It was not until May 1866, that Dodge reappeared in Omaha to take over the job that he would push to the finish. It was no particular disappointment to the engineer to find that he was starting from scratch. Ground had been broken, with the help of bursts of oratory from George Francis Train, but no grade had been built. At least the newcomer could be free to make his own mistakes.

One point had been settled: the line of the road was to be up the valley of the Platte and over the continental divide at the "best point available." Buffalo and Indians had shown the way somewhere near the present line of U.S. Highway 40 in southern Wyoming. The fur traders knew it and the Mormons had gone that way under the guidance of Jim Bridger, who had built his post at what he was sure would be a good spot for trade. Gold hunters traveled it and the wagons of emigrants bound for Oregon or California had marked it. There were names along the way that were almost as familiar as the streets of the towns from which the wanderers came — Brady's Island, where a lone trapper had made his last stand, Courthouse Rock, Chimney Rock, Independence Rock, on which men from the covered wagons had scratched initials and a date, Devil's Gate, Fort Bridger, Pacific Springs, and many more all the way to Fort Hall and beyond. Fort Hall on the Snake River was a favorite dividing point separating the Oregon-bound from those who chose California.

Later Dodge expressed his preference for the Snake River Route continuing down the Columbia to Fort Vancouver, practically the present route of the Oregon Short Line from Salt Lake City to the Northwest. This opinion of Dodge's was little more than an *obiter dictum*. Congress had tied Omaha to California in 1862 and the Californians were on their way up the western slope of the Sierras to meet the Union Pacific.

Buffalo and fur traders and emigrants do not necessarily show the way for rails and steam. Dodge knew this and he knew the country east of the divide. When he had waited in Council Bluffs before the war he had freighted from Council Bluffs to the hustling mining camp that was to become the city of Denver. This infant metropolis now took it for granted that the railroad, when and as built, would of course come by way of Denver. Motorists who have made the long climb over the eleven thousand foot summit of Berthoud Pass or Loveland can understand why one look at the high mountains back of

Denver led the engineering mind to conclude that a long look elsewhere was indicated. South Pass beyond the Black Hills had been no problem for wagon wheels, but steam demanded an easier grade for the approach on the eastern slope.

That was found and the manner of the finding illustrated the difficulties that surveyors and graders must face with Indians. This was the hunting ground of hard riding, hard fighting Sioux, Cheyennes, and Arapahoes and the Indians would defend their land with all they had. Here was a problem that did not hamper the California builders. Their Indians, mostly Paiute or Shoshone, were peaceful and easily conciliated. Crocker and Huntington gave orders that chiefs were to be permitted to ride free in smoking cars when trains began to run and lesser tribesmen were allowed on freights. No such petty overtures would satisfy the Sioux warriors. They were playing for keeps and they seemed to understand that there was not room enough on the plains for war ponies and iron horses. Troops were detailed to guard work gangs, moving grizzled old Indian fighter George Crook to comment scornfully on the railroad idea that each soldier on foot should surround three Indians on horseback. Sherman first discounted the Indian menace as of little importance. A swarm of railroad workers would mean enough whiskey to kill all the Indians within three hundred miles, he said. Evidently the general overestimated the effective range of construction camp whiskey or Indian capacity was greater than he thought. In the end it was the workers themselves who did most of the fighting. They were largely Civil War veterans seasoned under Grant and Sherman, willing to drop pick and shovel and take up musket without waste of time.

When the builders of the Northern Pacific were heading into the Sioux country of the Dakotas and Montana in the seventies after the Little Big Horn fight they borrowed the Central Pacific expedient and improved on it by issuing standing orders that all Indians, whether chiefs or not, were to be permitted to ride free on both passenger and freight trains. The Indians were not slow to seize the chance for joy rides and trainmen and passengers were treated to the spectacle of hard riding warriors seated on cushions or on top of freight cars viewing the scenery from such comfortable posts. When they had seen enough the free riders would drop off and catcñ the next train back. This was safer than fighting and a lot more fun. Soon they were supporters of the railroad instead of battlers against it.

In the sixties the Indians of the High Plains and the eastern slope of the Rockies had reason to worry. The fur traders in the early decades of the century had given them little trouble and in reality the traders had brought profit to them. The posts had provided a market for their desultory pelts and post whiskey was not hard to find if they knew how to look fot it. The Mountain Men were usually friendly, at least with the young squaws, and often useful in skirmishes with the hated Blackfeet. There were few of them and as a rule the proud Sioux and Arapahoes refused to take a handful of trappers seriously. The covered wagon people furnished amusement for young warriors itching to collect white scalps and count coup on these stupid, helpless people who dragged along at the pace set by their plodding oxen. The Argonauts were more serious and gold strikes in Wyoming, Montana, and Colorado hinted at more permanent inroads. California, followed closely by Nevada, set the braves in motion, many of them with guns that they had stolen or bought from shifty traders.

Now came curious men who peered through long tubes and drove stakes in the ground. At first they were merely amusing to the red men and their stakes made better fires than buffalo chips. But the "long lookers" kept coming to drive more stakes. There were rumors among the Pawnees to the eastward that there were other white men, many of them, digging holes in the ground and setting high poles on which they were stringing wires. Still more foolish whites were digging up the prairie and piling up the dirt in long ridges. It was all very mysterious and perhaps something should be done about it so the Northern Cheyennes, always friendly with the Sioux, joined in for the doing.

Horses stolen or strayed from Spanish explorers long ago, in the time of Coronado, had changed these plains people from feeble, half starved beggars to well fed, hard riding horsemen, the best light cavalry in the world they were to be called. These fighters were not to be ignored or bought off as were the Paiutes and Shoshones of Nevada and California. So the long wars began.

For Dodge there was an interval between the Civil War and building the Union Pacific. He was still considering the problem of a practicable route up the eastern slope of the Divide, but his immediate job was a campaign against the Sioux in the region of the Yellowstone. This little war was short and indecisive and Dodge was on his way back to the main command. This was in 1865. He had become separated from his small patrol along a ridge around the head of what he called Lone Tree Creek and there were hostiles at his heels. Riding hard he made his way back to his troops, but in doing this he realized that the grade down which he was riding was easier than he had expected. For a few minutes he was a surveyor and no longer an army officer riding for his life. In his final report after the railroad was built and the Indian menace no longer present he recalled his thought in that desperate moment: "If we saved our scalps I believed we had found a railroad line over the mountains." That was the way the rails went, and not over the South Pass that the Overland stages and the emigrant wagons had known. Today its name is Sherman Summit, but the surveyors knew it as Lone Tree Hill.

For the builders of the Union Pacific the whole stretch of country from the first crossing of the Platte to the meeting with the Central Pacific at Promontory Point held the possibility of Indian attack, and graders and tracklayers became soldiers at a moment's notice. One attack was staged within sight of the head of track. One of the frequent commissions had just pulled in in their special car when the sound of gunfire announced other visitors. In the flurry of fighting that followed the members of the commission caught up guns and joined in to good purpose.

At another time word came for Dodge at Plum Creek that Sioux riders had captured a work train behind him. Dodge had twenty free riders in his work car, clerks, tracklayers, casual visitors, all strangers to Dodge. As he headed back for the relief of the beleaguered train he called for volunteers. All of them stepped forward and when they arrived at the danger spot this mixed lot of volunteers deployed as skirmishers and soon sent the raiders hunting for cover. Railroad worker and war veteran were synonymous terms on the U.P.

When Dodge reached Council Bluffs to take over his post, time was running out, time that Credit Mobilier had wasted in political intrigue and inside maneuver. Now there was little room for an orderly sequence of surveying, grading, tracklaying. Instead graders were crowding on the heels of the surveyors. Until the first crossing of the Platte near Brady's Island the surveyors had easy going. The terrain was level and Indians gave little trouble. This was country that Dodge had seen before and the route was fixed and ready for the grading and tracklaying gangs. Trouble for everybody came with the approach to the mountains; trouble, that is, for everybody but the financial people who saw larger subsidies waiting in the mountain country. Part of the government plan for financing the line was the guaranteeing of railroad bonds as sections were approved by the government representatives. The amount of bonds thus secured varied with the terrain, $16,000 a mile for level ground; then $32,000 in broken country, and up to $48,000 in the mountains.

Foreseeing argument over the definition of a mountain, especially when $32,000 a mile might well depend on the choice of a dictionary, Congress in the Act of 1862, after laying down the basic terms of the guarantee as $16,000 per mile, went on to provide for the sections of unusual difficulty:

> That for three hundred miles of said road most mountainous and difficult of construction, to wit: one hundred and fifty miles westerly from the eastern base of the Rocky Mountains, and one hundred and fifty miles eastwardly from the western base of the Sierra Nevada Mountains . . . . the bonds to be issued to aid in the construction thereof shall be treble the number hereinbefore provided . . . ; and between the sections last named of one hundred and fifty miles each the bonds to be issued to aid in the construction thereof shall be double the number first mentioned.

For all the congressional caution, however, the shrewd Californians found a way to move mountains to serve their purposes. Arcade Creek, not far from Sacramento, displayed soil of a color that had some resemblance to disintegrated granite. This, said the lords of the Big Four, is where the mountains begin. It was also the beginning of the $48,000 bonus, although it was at least twenty-four miles before there was genuine sign of the foothills, a mere trifle of $768,000 on the right side of the Central Pacific ledger.

Dodge knew better than anyone else the problems that lay ahead of him if he was to match miles and subsidies with the Central Pacific. From the Missouri to the Golden Gate was approximately two thousand miles, and they were not ordinary miles. Tentative surveys had begun, at least for reconnaissance, but Durant's offhand assurance that buffalo and Indians had

long since marked the route to follow over the Rockies was
more cheering than accurate. Stuart and his men carrying reports to Astor had found their way over South Pass more than
half a century earlier, but the game trails they had followed
in their slow climb up from the west to the dry plateau of the
Pass had been a series of guesses, good and bad, and the same
could be said of the drop to the level of the Platte at the eastern end. Rails demanded easier grades if operating costs were
to be kept within reason. Dodge was sure he had found an
approach at the east as he rode hard down the slope to save his
scalp, but the western approach was yet to be determined.
Stuart had made his way up the Columbia and along the Snake,
but the railroad was being aimed for the basin of Great Salt
Lake and on to the gold fields of Nevada. Somewhere in that
long hard stretch they were to "meet and connect" with the
rails creeping over the Sierras.

CHAPTER XIII

Bringing Rails to Railhead

BOTH EAST and west there were hard problems of material. The treeless plains from Omaha to the Rockies provided no timber for ties or bridges and no stone. At the Central Pacific end the Sierras were more generous with timber especially on the western slope, but the stone was mostly a hard granite difficult to work. In the Rockies there was stone but few large trees for bridge timber except in the nearby Wasatch. Both roads must look to the remote East for rails and rolling stock.

From the beginning transport was a constant torment, slower and more expensive for the Californians. Around Cape Horn was the cheapest, $17.50 a ton laid down in San Francisco, but it was also by far the slowest, at least twice as long and more if head winds off the Cape were more stubborn than usual. The cost of transshipping rails and heavy equipment over the lift of twenty-five miles across the Isthmus sometimes ran to $5.00 a ton plus the cost of unloading and reloading in Panama, and the deadly yellow jack took its toll of the workers; time was more valuable than men when there was a railroad to build. In New York Huntington was straining his credit to the breaking point, but his angry persistence paid dividends. He was able to get ships for his cargoes when other would-be shippers could get only promises. In California gold was the circulating medium that everybody wanted. The maligned greenbacks dropped to 30 per cent of their face value and many refused them at that. At one time Hopkins consulted Huntington on the advisability of taking his salary in Central Pacific stock. Huntington's reply was a trifle cryptic: "Take as much as you can, but no more than you must."

For the Union Pacific material came up the Missouri from St. Louis and by work train and horsepower to railhead. That was changed when rails reached Omaha from the Mississippi in November 1867, although even then schedules were uncertain and delays frequent, but seldom long. At railhead the sole motive power was horses and mules, sometimes as many as ten thousand. In all six million ties were needed and three hundred thousand tons of rails. Prices of the simplest necessities were fantastic: wood for fuel, a hundred dollars a cord; grain, seven dollars a bushel; hay, thirty dollars a ton.

It can be said that both railroads were built by hand work, Chinese in California, under the driving impetus of Charlie Crocker. On the Union Pacific end there were many Irish, most of them ex-soldiers, sometimes almost equaling the four-footed workers in numbers. Dodge was fortunate in his choice of men to head the construction gangs, two brothers, General Jack and Dan Casement. Jack, who had commanded a division in the Army of the West in the Civil War, was now a tough driver of the work gangs at railhead. Dan was the man who saw to it that the material kept flowing up from the base as fast as it was needed. The Casement brothers would be heard from often as the work went on.

Dodge with his combined training in railroad building and war saw to it that his survey parties were organized and trained for their exacting work. More than once surveyors were hard put to it to keep ahead of the graders and tracklayers, especially on the easy going of the flat country. A typical survey party would be eighteen or twenty men: a chief, two assistants, rodmen, chainmen, flagmen, and in game country a hunter. When Indians were expected a guard of ten or more soldiers would be added. Even with soldier guards more than one surveyor lost his scalp. In 1867, one survey gang found itself without a leader when its chief L. L. Hills was killed by Indians. In this crisis young J. M. Eddy, an axman who had enlisted in the 13th Illinois at the age of sixteen by skilful juggling of dates, took charge and brought the others to Camp Collins, the railhead of the moment. Dodge promoted him and he stayed with the railroad company to become general manager of the Southwestern System.

As they came up on Laramie Plains surveyors and builders alike were tormented by the lack of pure water. From Laramie west alkali was the rule and often fresh water must be brought a hundred miles or more in improvised tank cars. Of the well-named Bitter Creek desert the grim jest was that jack rabbits crossing it carried knapsacks and canteens. One engineer reported a stretch of sixty miles in the Utah desert without drinkable water and suggested the use of camels by survey crews. To find a spring of fresh water near the line was an event of such importance that General John Rawlins, one of the location engineers, declared that if anything were ever named for him he hoped it would be a spring; his wish came true and the thriving little city of Rawlins, Wyoming, with a present population of approximately nine thousand was the result.

In the settled country of the eastern states the surveys were simplified by the fact that the general location of the line was easily determined. From Albany to Buffalo was an obvious route as was the line from New York to Boston or

Philadelphia. Now these two roads, groping painfully toward each other, were confronted by a tangle of mountains and canyons, rivers that were dry today and raging torrents tomorrow, stretches of alkali plains with blazing hot summers and killing storms in winter. Little was known of the natural resources of the different regions except as army topographers may have had a look. Dodge was particularly concerned with possible deposits of minerals, especially coal for the engines. Signs of gold and silver were found and what was more important to Dodge was a bed of lignite five to ten feet thick was struck near the U.P. line in the Medicine Bow region of Wyoming.

Days were spent and miles traveled combing country that would never see a mile of rails laid. The chief engineer's report of 1868 showed 3,310 miles of reconnaissance survey for the year for which more than five thousand miles of travel by surveyors had been required. One estimate made after the road was finished claimed that the exploratory trips amounted to twenty-five thousand miles and that fifteen thousand miles of experimental line had been run by the engineers in locating the final line of 1,095 miles to the meeting place with the Central Pacific at Promontory Point on the Great Salt Lake.

As the engineers groped and sighted and measured and drove their stakes the graders and tracklayers pressed close on their heels. The first short year gave the workers little more than the semblance of a start, forty miles, but the next year, 1866, saw 250 miles built and approved. The year they crossed the Continental Divide, 1867, gave them almost as much mileage in spite of mountains and canyons. From the summit of the Rockies at an altitude of close to eight thousand feet it became more and more each day a race against the Central Pacific with a glittering prize of government subsidy and land grant bonds for the winner. In spite of the pressure un-

der which they worked the surveyors found time to swing
wide around a broken wagon tire marking the grave of Re-
becca Winters who reached the end of her trail to Oregon somewhere east of South Pass. The last lap from April 1868 to
May 1869 added up to 555 miles.

The construction crews under Jack Casement were town-
builders, policemen, Indian fighters as well as railroad builders. Each new railhead called for a camp with living quarters
for the men. Sometimes these lasted only a few weeks or for
a summer. Sometimes a town emerged that was there to stay.
That was the way Cheyenne and Laramie were born. A common term for the short-lived cluster of huts, saloons, dance
halls, and honkytonks that sprang up at each new railhead
was "Hell on Wheels." A few years later such a town on the
Northern Pacific rushing toward the coast was christened
"Hell to Pay." It still lives as a whistle stop in eastern Washington with the chaste name of "Eltopia."

The gamblers and toughs who moved forward with the
builders had valiant competition from the Casements. Part
of the Casement standard equipment was a portable, knock-
down building that was a combination of warehouse, store,
dining-room and bunkhouse, a center of railroad activity while
it lasted; then it traveled on to the next railhead. There was
bickering over a division point east of the Divide. Dodge had
chosen Cheyenne and by July 1867, the sale of lots was going
forward briskly. The price at the beginning was two hundred
and fifty dollars a lot, soon rising to six hundred. Before the
first boom ended as much as thirty-five hundred per lot was
asked and it was reported that the first year sixty thousand
dollars had been received in down payments. Then Vice-President Durant, viewing this tempting bonanza from afar, forgot his promise of a free hand to Dodge, and announced that
the division point had been shifted to Laramie, having ad-

vised a group of his friends that large profits lay in Laramie real estate. Dodge was in Washington and took thought of his own friends who had bought early and often in Cheyenne. He demanded a showdown and carried his grievances to Grant and Sherman who knew him from war days. It was Durant who was forced to back down and make his peace as best he could with his trusting friends. Both towns lived to become good communities, as the census figures for 1960 show: Cheyenne, 43,505; Laramie, 17,520. In the year of its birth Cheyenne boasted a branch bank, a post office ten feet by fifteen and a saloon, the Headquarters, thirty-six feet by a hundred. There were also two daily papers and a brass band, and of course hotels, gambling rooms, and dance halls. Altogether quite a lusty yearling.

Julesberg was one town that was there before the railroad came. It was a division point and a meal stop on the Overland stage route with the reputation of being the "Wickedest Town in America," named for one Jules remembered only for his prowess with the six-shooter. He seems to have met the fate of most western bad men, that of running into another gunman faster and trickier than himself. In the case of Brother Jules that was a man named Slade. Slade took over Jules's job of division agent on the Overland and proved his ability by cleaning out the "road agents" who had been holding up stages. The contagion of killing is irresistible and Slade soon could boast a bloodier record than Jules had made.

Knowing the old reputation of the place the railroad thoughtfully bypassed the old Julesberg decreeing a new one at what they thought was a safe distance; but it was not too far for the gamblers and gunmen. In June the population of the new town was forty men and one woman; by the end of July there were four thousand men and women, many of them with itchy forefingers. Dodge sent the reliable Jack Casement to

put the place in order and in the fall Jack reported to his
chief that the troublemakers had decided to go elsewhere, several to the town cemetery, leaving only the station agent in
moderate health. Five months later the station agent had gone
and Julesberg was quiet at last. There is still a town of that
name hardly more than a whistle stop on the Union Pacific
schedules, and there is no gunplay.

In May 1868, J. E. House, division engineer at Cheyenne,
reported to Dodge that he had already located a dozen towns
each with half a section of land, three hundred and twenty
acres, staked for railroad use; O'Fallon, Alkali, Ogallala, Big
Spring, Julesberg, Lodge Pole, Sidney, Potter, Antelope, Pine
Bluffs, Hillsdale, Cheyenne. Railroad builders east of the Mississippi and north of the Ohio had found towns ready and
waiting for them. Beyond the Missouri rails led the westward
march. It was a favorite tale among western railroad operators
that freight trains crossing the flat country east of the Rockies kept a brakeman stationed on the rear platform of the
waycar to report towns that he saw spring up after the train
had passed.

Towns that stayed after rails pushed on west, as many
did, soon organized courts and administered a rough and ready
justice. In one such case the judge announced a standard pen-
alty for gunplay, hit or miss alike, ten dollars and two bits.
An inquisitive spectator inquired "Why the two bits?" His
Honor snapped back: "To buy your honorable judge a drink
in the morning." On another occasion a committee of the local vigilantes gave a trouble maker "fifteen minutes to leave
town. There's your mule." The gunman gave them bland assurance: "Thanks, gentlemen. If the mule don't buck five's
plenty." Out of such a life grew the slogan long current among
Western railroaders: "West of the Mississippi there is no Sun-
day; west of the Missouri there is no God."

Stories of life in the Far West were never conservative, farms and towns did spring up in the wake of the railroad at a surprising rate, and life in that raw country was not easy. Nevertheless by the end of 1867 the Episcopal church authorities could boast fourteen churches in the diocese of Nebraska. Other denominations, Methodist and Baptist especially, were generally better known for their missionary enterprise than was the Episcopal so it is fair to assume that their figures would be more impressive. Clearly the amenities of life followed close on the heels of the railroad builders.

In the westward march schools and colleges traveled with towns and churches. Before Denver had really risen above the status of a mining camp in 1861 a state university was established at nearby Boulder and in 1864 the University of Denver appeared. Kansas claimed a state agricultural school in 1863 and a state medical school in 1865, and the year that saw rails dip over the Continental Divide, 1867, also witnessed the establishment of a state teachers college at Peru, Nebraska. There were bleak years ahead for railroads and colleges, but the once Wild West was settling into its stride. Gang plows and diplomas were taking the place of broncos and sixguns.

Early in the game, October 1866, the irrepressible Durant, irritated by the unwillingness of Eastern capital to buy subsidy bonds or railroad stock, staged a special excursion to give the Easterners a view of the work under way, a trainload of dignified gentlemen in high silk hats and charming ladies in Paris gowns. Elaborate preparations were made with dining and dancing and much champagne. Dodge had a sense of humor and a touch of Western swagger. Early in the morning when the visitors were sound asleep he alerted Major North and his Pawnee scouts and sent them riding and yelling and firing their guns in a fake raid on the innocent visitors. There was tumult and screams that were not fakes. When Dodge appeared

the scouts rode back to their camp, and the Indian war ended with a gargantuan breakfast in the early dawn. Durant
announced that the financial log jam had been broken and
the excursionists went back to their banks and their drawing-
rooms to tell tales of life in the Far West. There were other
excursions later, after the trains began to run, men and wom-
en looking for land riding as guests of the railroad, the seller
of land, but none quite like this curtain raiser.

CHAPTER XIV

The Dream Fulfilled

THERE might be time at the Omaha base for champagne and oratory and horseplay; at railhead there was time only for work and a spot of Indian fighting that was not stage play. Rails came up to the end of track on flat cars drawn by horses over the last stretch. Driving the horses gave jobs for boys who delighted in the rush and the noise. Brawny arms lifted the rails from the car, six or eight men to a rail, working usually at a run. Spikes were driven at the same headlong pace, ten to a rail, three blows of the sledge for each spike. W. A. Bell, an amateur statistician, summarized the tracklaying procedure: "There are ten spikes to a rail, four hundred rails per mile, eight hundred miles to San Francisco — 21,000,000 sledge blows to the Coast." Men died or dropped out. Other men took their places. The rails pushed steadily westward, a mile a day, sometimes on the good days three miles or more. They were tough men, hard fighting, drinking, swearing, gambling, as good with their guns as with their sledges and they laid the rails over the mountains and down into the Salt Lake basin.

From the top of the Rockies on this became each day more of a race with the Central Pacific for the grand prize of $64,000 in subsidy bonds per mile plus 12,800 acres of land. Now the Union Pacific was really moving. That year of 1867 was a tough one for their rivals in the Sierras. They could report only forty miles of rails laid; it was five years since the first shovelfuls had been dug at Sacramento and the Union Pacific had beaten them six times over in miles for the year.

From Sacramento to the summit was only a hundred and five miles but they were uphill miles, a rise of 7,012 feet to the ridgepole of the Sierras. There were ten tunnels to be cut through hard granite, more work for the patient Orientals. The last bore through the summit itself was 1,659 feet long. In the Dutch Flat country there were old gold camps that the Forty-niners had christened Gold Run, Red Dog, You Bet, Little York. As though in a spirit of revulsion the Central Pacific chose names for stations that suggest the taste of a romantic woman novelist of the period: Oreana, Winnemucca, Golconda, Beowawe, Cluro, Fungi. Fantastic as the names were some of the towns lived.

There were many doubters, East and West alike, who scoffed at the idea of a practicable railroad in such country. The deep snow in the Sierras alone would make operation impossible; ten to fifteen feet were not uncommon and fifty-foot drifts not unknown. On the western slope men measured snow in feet not inches. The builders met that threat with thirty-seven miles of wooden snowsheds, enabling the trains to run under cover. Snow is a seasonable hazard on any railroad through high mountains, as the Union Pacific was to discover in the first year of operation. Half a dozen trains were stalled on Laramie Plain long enough to necessitate the bringing in of supplies on sledges and snowshoes. In one of the cars there was an opera company bound for San Francisco and the members gallantly proceeded to give performances for the snowbound travelers in spite of the limitations of space and the crudity of the lighting arrangements.

There were prophets of glory as well as of doom. In 1868 a railroad report pointed to the potential wealth of the Pacific slope. Now with only a million inhabitants the annual output of gold was fifty to sixty million dollars with wheat, vegetables, and hides to boot. "Population will pour over it in a steady stream until the million of inhabitants become six millions and the wealth of the country is multiplied ten-fold." (The census of 1960 shows a total of 15,717,204.) For once the facts of today make the promotional flight look modest. Substitute oil for gold and the wealth of California seems sidereal compared with the most extravagant estimates. And not oil only but annual crops of fruit and vegetables. Name almost any variety and the odds are heavy that California leads all the states year by year. A county in the San Joaquin valley shows more cotton in a year than any comparable area in the country. Another county, Santa Clara, probably "grows the lettuce that feeds the world." Motorists entering the town of Watsonville not too far from where Leland Stanford built his university are confronted with this sign: "Welcome to Watsonville, the Artichoke Capital of the World!" The harvest of gold and oil can be gathered only once. Fruit and vegetables require no "depletion allowance."

Surveyors for both lines were poking into the Salt Lake basin and early in the summer of 1868 rival crews met in Echo Canyon looking for a way through the Wasatch Mountains. Now they were in Mormon country and Salt Lake City was less than a hundred miles away. The Mormon country, "outside the United States," had been pierced. The invading engineers were surprised to meet their rivals there, but it was no surprise to Brigham Young. He had seen the railroads coming for months and was ready for them. He at least knew what good politicians know when tough opposition confronts them, "If you can't beat 'em, jine 'em." Brigham had failed to escape from the United States so now he made the best of it. In the hard years of their great migration he had sent five hundred of his young men to fight against Mexico. That was a hedge against the future. Now twenty years later he was ready with a bid of two million dollars to build the line from the Wasatch to Salt Lake City, thus making sure of railroad service for his people.

It was not quite that simple. The engineer's reports showed that the route through Ogden to skirt the north shore of Salt Lake was cheaper to build and to maintain. Dodge stood pat on the survey figures which showed that a route on the south side of the lake by Salt Lake City meant fifteen miles on a ninety-foot grade against the north side with five miles at eighty feet.

Young fumed and preached a bitter sermon in the Tabernacle against Dodge, declaring that the road could not be built or operated without Mormon aid. He would throw his support to the Central Pacific people who could tell the difference between a hawk and a handsaw. When the Central Pacific engineers agreed with Dodge on the route Young went back to the U.P. side and reinstated his construction bid. While the fulminations and arguments went on surveyors and tracklayers for both roads rushed on to increase the mileage and the subsidy.

The meeting of rival survey gangs in Echo Canyon had given added impetus to the spirit of rivalry and both roads were driving hard to outspace each other. The vagueness of the Act of 1862 and the failure of authority in Washington to declare a definite junction point gave the tracklayers a free hand as Irish confronted Oriental in the Utah desert.

It has never been made quite clear who, if anyone, decided that the meeting place of Central and Union Pacific should be at Promontory Point on the Great Salt Lake. In Washington the Secretary of the Interior, not an engineer or a tracklayer, told a committee of Congress that the junction was "assumed to be" 78.295 miles east of Salt Lake City. Graders and tracklayers knew nothing about decimal fractions; their concern was with miles and days and they pushed on. When the Central gangs reached the point that is now Reno, Nevada, home of easy divorce and high play, they found there a total of two men, one woman, three pigs, and a cow, but in a week there were thirty new buildings and Charlie Crocker whipped up the pace of his Chinese reliables. As the Union Pacific came down hill to meet the Central they too gathered impetus and rival grading crews overlapped, pausing only long enough to exchange epithets and volleys of stones. By 1960 Reno admitted to a population of 51,470.

It was exciting of course while it lasted a mixture of high melodrama and low comedy, but it was no way to build a railroad. Probably it was the absurdity of this competition that forced a compromise on Promontory Point. As a sporting event it was a draw, but the U.P. could claim a victory in miles built: 1,086 miles from Omaha to the junction against 689 for the C.P. from Sacramento. The C.P. could claim a different kind of victory, over the altitude and steep slopes of the Sierras with a tunnel to drive through the stubborn granite of the summit. And taking rails down the eastern slope of that towering range was no child's play for all Judah's offhand assurance that the task presented no serious difficulties.

Many years later two Canadian railroads were to face a slightly different kind of rivalry and were to reach a less happy solution. In that case Grand Trunk Pacific and Canadian

Northern were racing neck and neck for Yellowhead Pass on the way to Prince Rupert on the Pacific. Grand Trunk surveyors got there first and of course the best location at the lower level leaving the Canadian Northern no alternative but to cut a right of way along the steep mountainside above the Grand Trunk. To dispose of the rubble from the blasts chutes were run out over the rival's right of way. Bankruptcy hung over both lines and as a result the Canadian government took over and today the Canadian National, government owned and operated, runs the trains to Prince Rupert.

When a compromise junction was agreed to, "somewhere near Ogden," as the official record declared, plans were made for appropriate ceremony and celebration. But before that happened there was one last big day of tracklaying, twelve hours and ten miles of track. The names of the men who carried the rails that day are revealing: Mike Shay, Mike Sullivan, Mike Kennedy, Pat Joyce, Thomas Dailey, George Wyatt, Edward Killeen, Fred McNamara. The weight of the rails they carried in the twelve hours was 1,970,000 pounds. The date set for the final blow that should unite East and West was May 19, 1869. It has been said of the Union Pacific that it took thirty years to plan and six years to build. This is less than fair to the builders. Of these building years only four really counted and on that day in May the tracklayers could look back on 1,100 miles laid in four years and one month, all carried and laid by hand.

The top brass of both roads was of course present at the finish to applaud, make speeches, drink, and get in the way of the workers. The delegation from the East, chiefly New York and Washington, had a longer trip to make to reach the scene and storms had additionally delayed them. Near the Divide a strike of train crews whose payday was overdue slowed them still more, so that the California special was forced to wait two days. Fortunately their cars were warm and well supplied with the necessary palliatives.

Finally the moment came, the engines of the two specials stood nose to nose, the speeches had been made, the last tie and the last spike was ready. The tie was of native laurel, carefully selected, eight feet long, eight inches wide, and six inches deep. A silver plate announced to posterity: "The Last Tie Laid on the Completion of the Pacific Railroad," with the date and the names of officials concerned with the building. Tie and silver plate were taken up after the ceremony and deposited in a museum in San Francisco where they were burned in the great fire of 1906.

The famous golden spike made of twenty dollar gold pieces is still in existence as is the silver sledge used in the driving. In fact there was an oversupply of last spikes, one of silver from the Comstock lode in Virginia City, one of gold from Idaho, and a mixture of gold, silver, and iron from Montana and California. Stanford had the honor of the first blow, missing the spike entirely. There were other dignitaries to try their luck and finally the spike was driven home by the chief engineers of the two roads.

Unfortunately for posterity there were no cameras, radio or television to record what was said and done. A telegraph operator reported the successive blows with "Done!" for the last one, but the dots and dashes of the Morse Code provided little drama for the distant audience. Dodge in his official report mentions the weather, windy and raw, and concludes: "After a few speeches we all took refuge in the Central Pacific cars where wine flowed freely and many speeches were made." In San Francisco impromptu parades were organized when word came over the wire that the last spike was set and among the improvised banners and transparencies was one declaring "California annexes the United States!"

The spectacle of the two locomotives, pilot to pilot, moved Francis Bret Harte to break into verse in the *Overland Monthly* "What Was It the Engines Said?" Unfortunately his muse seemed unequal to the drama of the occasion and after a promising first stanza lapsed into a thin rendering of Western dialect. The first and last stanzas are offered here as evidence:

> What was it the engines said
> Pilots touching — head to head,
> Facing on the single track
> Half a world behind each back?
> This is what the engines said,
> Unreported and unread.
>
>   *   *   *   *   *
>
> Said the Union, "Don't reflect or
> I'll run over some Director."
> Said the Central, "I'm Pacific
> But when riled I'm quite terrific.
> Yet today we shall not quarrel,
> Just to show these folks this moral,
> How two engines in their vision
> Once have met without collision."
> This is what the engines said,
> Unreported and unread,
> Spoken slightly through the nose
> With a whistle at the close.

Now that the drinking and the speaking and the cheering were over the trainmen and the dispatchers and all the other servitors of steam went to work without delay. The next day, May 11, the first regular passenger train over the Union Pacific left Omaha and a day later a fast freight loaded with the new crop of China tea left San Francisco. Here was the fulfillment of an old dream of world trade, older than Astor with his plan for an empire of fur controlled from the stockade at the mouth of the Columbia when British, Russian, and Yankee skippers out of Boston had come close to war with the sea otter as the prize. In his report for 1868 General Dodge had emphasized the saving of time with the completion of the railroad link to the Coast, New York to Yokohama in thirty days against forty-five from London around the Cape of Good Hope to Shanghai. It was a brave hope and many cargoes of tea and silk were to roll from San Francisco to New York, but a French engineer, Ferdinand de Lesseps, had a better idea, a canal from the Mediterranean to the Red Sea, which was opened six months after the last spike was driven at Promontory Point.

We had yet to learn that railroads are empire builders and not merely bearers of burdens. When Lewis and Clark set off on their great adventure, the land west of the Mississippi was a savage waste fit only for Indians and there was much talk of making it a permanent Indian preserve; Jefferson's thrifty real estate deal with Napoleon was an act of folly. All he had bought was deserts and mountains. Talk of making it a part of the Union was the raving of madmen; the union of states belonged where it began along the Atlantic Coast. The census of 1800 showed only blanks for the trans-Mississippi country. Look at it now — more than forty million population in 1950 and still growing. The three states fronting the Pacific show more than fourteen million. All this and more in the making when East and West met at Promontory Point. Perhaps this was "What the Engines Said":

> Pilots touching — head to head,
> Facing on the single track
> Half a world behind each back!

INDEX

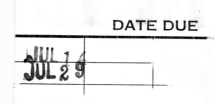